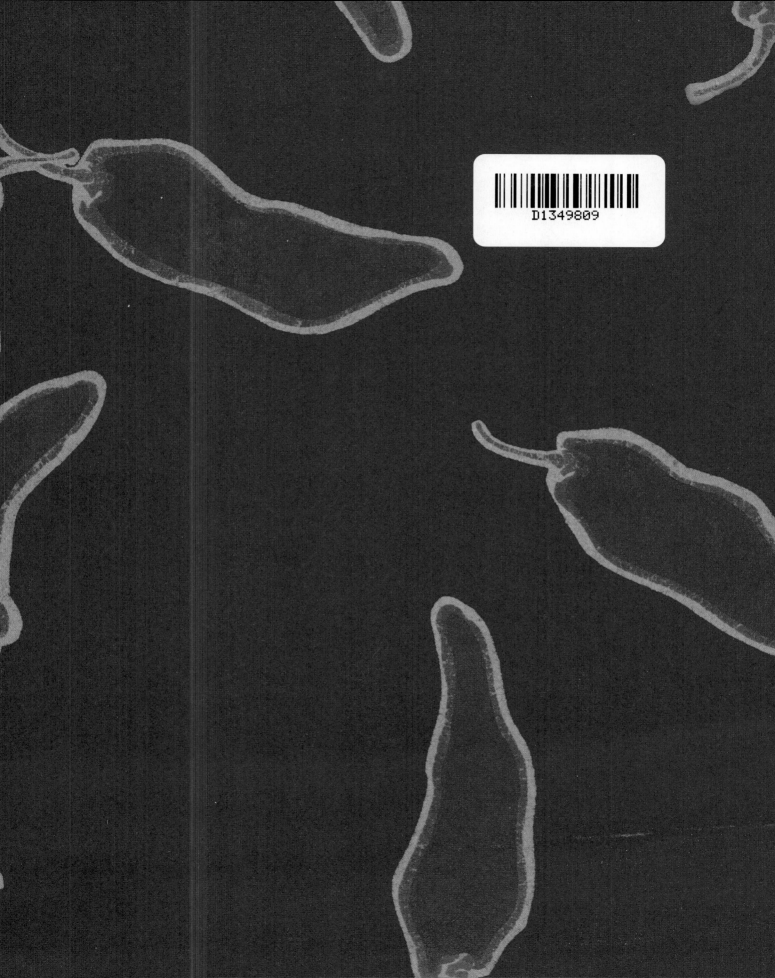

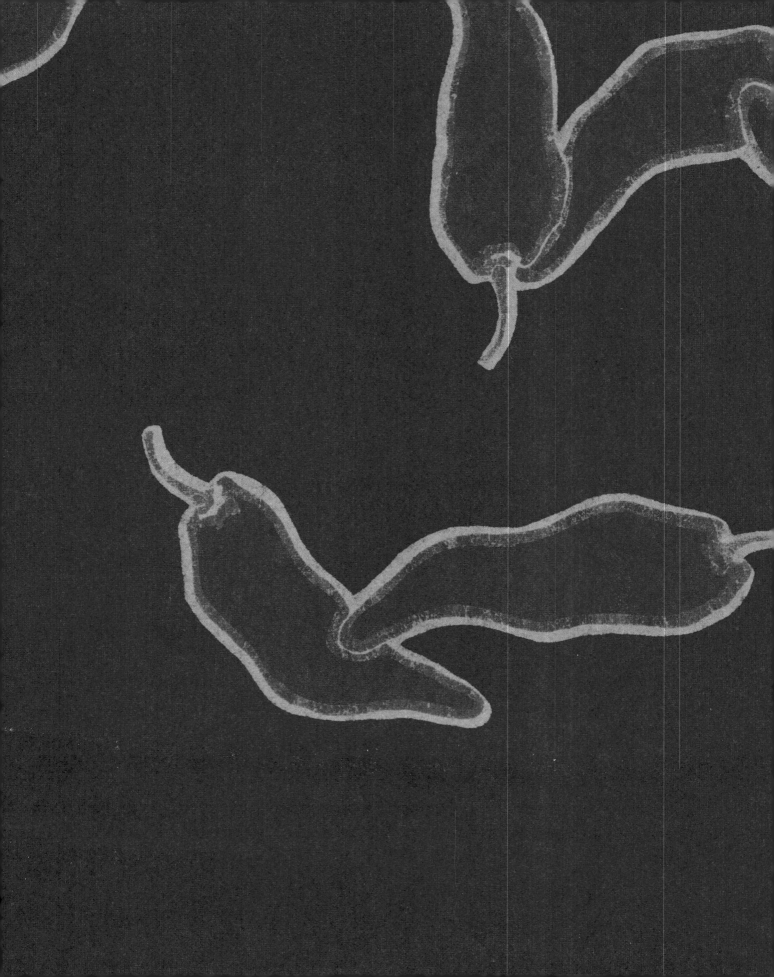

SPLENDID SETTINGS

The Art + Craft of Entertaining

Jane Korman

Foreword by David Revere McFadden

Contributions by Elisabeth Agro, Wendell Castle and Nancy Jurs, Toshiko Takaezu, and Betty Woodman

Proceeds from the sale of *Splendid Settings* will support
fellow research and education
in the Pulmonary and Critical Care Division of Medicine at
Thomas Jefferson University Hospital,
Philadelphia, Pennsylvania.

ISBN 978-0-9846243-0-0

www.splendidsettings.com

Photography by Stuart Goldenberg,
Patty Daniels, Sandy Gilvear, Jane
Korman, and Kim Sargent

Edited and designed by
Glenn Suokko

Copyediting by Catherine Melocik

Printed and bound at
Groupe PDI, Québec

Jacket: Samy D service and dinner
plates, Albert Paley iron-forged
candlesticks, Toshiko Takaezu
vessels

End papers: Fabric designed by
Mineo Mizuno and printed by the
Fabric Workshop and Museum

Page 1: Ken Ferguson pot

Page 2: Romulus Craft plates and
bowl, Micah Sherrill cup

page 4: Patrick Loughran plates
and bowls, Robert Mickelsen wine
glasses, Michael Schunke wine
glasses, Ginny Ruffner candlesticks,
Lisa Jenks salt and pepper shakers,
Mardi-Jo Cohen flatware

To my loving husband, Leonard,
who continues to make our journey through
the creative world the trip of a lifetime

Contents

Foreword

We may live without poetry, music, and art;

We may live without conscience, and live without heart;

We may live without friends; we may live without books;

But civilized man cannot live without cooks.

He may live without books,—what is knowledge but grieving?

He may live without hope,—what is hope but deceiving?

He may live without love,—what is passion but pining?

But where is the man that can live without dining?

So wrote the gourmand and one-time Viceroy of India Robert Bulwer-Lytton, 1st Earl of Lytton, in 1860. Sir Robert might well have penned these humorous lines after one of the many delightful lunches or dinners that Jane Korman has orchestrated so elegantly over the years.

This volume—at once a cookbook, guide to table settings and gracious entertaining, and autobiographical journal—invites the reader to join Jane at her own splendid table. Jane's book is a superb and tasty mayonnaise of ingredients harvested from two worlds—the world of cuisine and fine dining, and the world of art, craft, and design. Anyone who has had the good fortune of receiving an invitation to sup at Jane's table in Pennsylvania, New Jersey, or Florida takes away from the repast much more than a gratified palate. One's memories consist of seamlessly interwoven experiences of good food, good art, and, above all for the author, good friends.

I will never forget a dinner at Jane and Leonard's home in Pennsylvania in 2002, when the memories of 9/11 were still fresh in our minds and persistent in our dreams. Around a table of her guests—some, familiar friends; others, new acquaintances—we learned again why comfort food achieved its reputation as solace both for eager taste buds and stressed psyches. The humble masterpieces of the cook's repertoire were given center stage—nourishing meat loaf, creamy mashed potatoes, crisp salad, and a soothing chocolate bread pudding. Adding to the atmosphere was a masterful table setting: a choir of candlesticks of all shapes, sizes, and materials—glass, ceramic, metal—that created a flickering horizon of light down the middle of the table, symbolic lights of hope to remind us how important beauty is in our daily lives.

Intimate summertime lunches in Pennsylvania that concluded with brilliantly selected cheeses, delicious fig preserves, and a raspberry tart; and festive Florida dinner parties that turned a spotlight on treasures of the sea (along with unforgettable scalloped potatoes) were relished at various times in settings graced by the presence of imposing Cindy Sherman photographs, Warren McArthur's unique aluminum furniture, exuberant works in clay by Betty Woodman, and an unforgettable Petah Coyne wax sculpture.

The landscaping of the table—furnishing it with ceramics, glass, silver, flowers, and other amenities—has engaged designers for centuries. One need only think of the theatrical table settings created for the court dinners of Louis XV on one hand and of the elegantly understated refinement of the Japanese table on the other to recognize that the tabletop and the activities that surround it serve as a form of communication of both values and vision. They are, in fact, extensions of the personality of the host. Jane Korman's personality shines through on every page of this engaging and beautiful volume.

As a curator of decorative arts, craft, and contemporary art and design, I am convinced that Jane Korman and her style of entertaining are the proof of a pudding recipe that can only be mastered by those who know that art is not something extraneous to the rest of life. Those of us who are fortunate enough to count Jane as our friend have been the recipients of many pleasures and experiences that have enriched our lives and memories. Jane is an extraordinary woman whose friendship, talents, and intelligence are cherished and admired by her many friends and guests. Through this book, she invites a larger audience to become part of her world of art, food, and entertaining.

David Revere McFadden
Chief Curator
Museum of Arts and Design
New York, New York

Marek Cecula plates and bowls

Introduction

I LOVE PARTIES. I love to go to parties, but even more, I love to give parties.

My favorite thoughts while falling asleep are about planning menus and designing table settings for future parties. Better than counting sheep, thinking about menus and tables does the trick for me. In my mind, I create tables for a luncheon party under the shade of the trees in our garden in Pennsylvania or prepare an informal dinner on the deck of our beach house overlooking the ocean off the coast of New Jersey or set a festive table for a class reunion dinner in Florida.

My husband, Leonard, shares my love of art, design, and entertaining, and together we have planned and enjoyed countless meals over many years with family, friends, and guests. So it seemed only natural to write this book, *Splendid Settings: The Art + Craft of Entertaining,* to feature what I consider to be my most interesting and imaginative ideas for setting tables using our personal collections of dinnerware.

Splendid Settings is presented in four sections that are based on seasonal entertaining at our homes. The house we call home—in the countryside not far from Philadelphia, where we welcome each spring and celebrate the fall harvests and holidays—lends itself to formal place settings. CASUAL 111, our summer beach house in New Jersey, is where entertaining is just as the name of the house implies: casual. And the sunshine and tropical palm trees influence the table settings and menus created at our winter retreat in Florida. The recipes are a direct reflection of the four seasons, as well as the way we live and entertain at each location.

While stores are full of cookbooks written by outstanding food experts, this book is different: it shares my selection of treasured recipes alongside place settings and serving pieces that were made by contemporary craft artists whose work we have collected. The recipes are some of my favorites that I have referred to for years; some have been handed down to me from my mother and grand-mother, and some have been provided by dear friends who also love to cook. This book illustrates how I combine our collection of handmade contemporary crafts with traditional dinnerware and how the menu selection enhances the entire presentation. Although this is a personal story, I hope it will inspire others to create their own innovative table settings for lovely dinner parties, based on what they enjoy or collect.

Splendid Settings is meant to offer the reader menu and recipe suggestions that are uncomplicated and easy to prepare and suit today's relaxed lifestyle. Whether you choose to prepare a meal and present it in a simple or a formal setting, I'm sure you will agree that a beautiful table setting will always be appreciated by guests and contribute to the pleasure of even the simplest meal.

Alec Karros plates

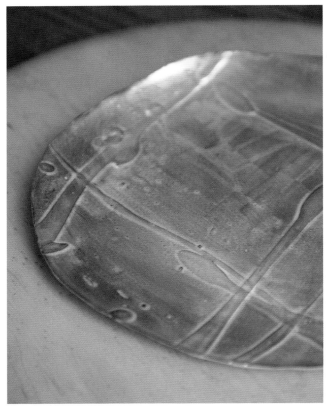

Yoshiaki Yuki charger

James Makins cup and saucer, creamer, and sugar; vintage dessert plate

Toshiko Takaezu closed-form vessels

Thank You

To my daughters, who have filled my life with joy beyond words and have always been there for me with enthusiasm, encouragement, and sound advice:

To Alison, who initially suggested compiling my craft stories and collections and combining them with favorite recipes in a publication—without your foresight, I would never have thought to write this book.

To Suzy, who spent days reorganizing my office and putting files in place while reading through countless chapters and testing many recipes—without your partnership and positive energy, I would never have gotten started.

And to Cathy, who, throughout the entire process, looked at the numerous photographs, identified the most interesting ones, and gave me a very objective and much appreciated review—your critical eye brought out the best this book could be.

To David Revere McFadden, chief curator of the Museum of Arts and Design, who graciously wrote the foreword to this book and whose friendship I will always treasure—your brilliant mind, discerning eye, and incredible memory for details never ceases to impress me.

To the team of Stuart Goldenberg and Barbara Botting for their exceptional photographs in Spring, Summer, and Fall and for their enthusiasm for this project.

To Kit Cornell—my "buddy" in the dreaming stage of this book, as well as in the kitchen—who has provided so many wonderful memories and meals for our family and friends.

To Nina Cioffi, who generously provided so many delicious recipes for our parties in Florida.

To Sandy Gilvear, who captured so joyfully with her camera all the fun in Florida in Winter. To Kim Sargent, who also contributed beautifully to the photography in Winter, and Patty Daniels, who took the wonderful photographs at the Work of Art party.

To my good friends Wendell Castle, Toshiko Takaezu, and Betty Woodman, whose work I adore and who contributed some of their favorite recipes, and Elisabeth Agro, for sharing through her cherished family recipe the sensitive story of her relationship with her mother-in-law.

To Glenn Suokko, my new BFF, who, from the moment we connected through the Internet, understood my vision for this book and, with his fine editing and design skills, created a beautiful result.

And especially to all the craftsmen whose work I have collected and enjoy. Their joy of the creative process as artists has translated into my joy in using handmade objects. Their spirit is always present at the party.

In Memoriam

To my mother, Rosalie, who taught me the importance of a life filled with the love of family and friends and the spiritual value of a beautifully set table.

Lisa Naples cups and saucers

Spring At Home in Pennsylvania

"I love Paris in the springtime," wrote Cole Porter. I'd change the title of that famous song to "I Love Pennsylvania in the Springtime." For over thirty years, Leonard and I have lived in a house we built on farmland twenty-five miles outside Philadelphia. From the first sight of crocuses pushing up through the ground to the opening blossoms of the crab apple and dogwood trees, azaleas, and rhododendrons, spring in this part of the country epitomizes the promise of a new season.

For me, May is a special month. When I was fifteen years old, May 2 was the day Leonard took me on our first date, to the high school play. And years later, May was the month that we moved into our dream house. Yes, I love springtime in Pennsylvania.

Our home in the country has been the site for many happy gatherings: family events, social evenings with friends, and parties for community and philanthropic endeavors. As our lives and interests evolve, we always find a reason to think about planning a new party with a different format. Traditional settings often take place in the dining room, while the gallery is a lovely place for an intimate luncheon with a museum curator, and the garden works perfectly for a museum committee luncheon.

In this chapter, I offer some of the most interesting combinations of table settings and springtime menus that have been enjoyed by our family and friends at our home in Pennsylvania.

Dan Dailey candlesticks

Wendell Castle demilune table
Dale Chihuly, *Macchia* series
Paul Soldner sculpture

Hooray for Daylight Saving Time

Nothing says "Spring is here!" better than daylight saving time, when the shifting of time is created for some regions around the globe to extend daylight in the afternoon by setting the clock ahead one hour. The first day we enjoy this welcome extension of daylight is a Sunday in March, and it is a perfect day for a casual celebration in the kitchen.

A splendid setting for the table is the polka–dot plates and bowls that I bought at a street fair in Santa Fe, New Mexico. The goblets by Pinkwater Glass can be turned upside down to use either the big or small bowl, depending on the choice of water or wine. The table is covered with multicolored scarves that are handwoven by Randall Darwall. Randall's palette shifts so no two inches of the scarves are alike. "Why use five colors when fifty will do nicely?" says this master weaver. Although I wear the scarves around my neck (one at a time, of course), several of them make a perfect tabletop covering when used as overlapping runners. The ceramic rooster holding fresh herbs in the center of the table is by Beatrice Wood and signed "Beato." Wood was a creative icon who combined the influence of Dada and folk art in her luster-glazed pots and figures; the evidence is clearly seen in her *Rooster with Cat*, dated 1978.

Randall Darwall handwoven scarves

Beatrice Wood, *Rooster with Cat*

Plate and bowl from a street fair

Pinkwater Glass goblets

Sicilian Caponata

Serves 12

While on a trip to Italy with four of our grandchildren, we had the ideal opportunity to take part in a private cooking lesson on a farm that boasted a fine cook. An Italian interpreter translated the quantities and ingredients into English for us as we took notes. After the lesson, we sat at the cook's farm table and enjoyed the dishes we helped her prepare. Our favorite dish was Sicilian Caponata, which I have enjoyed re-creating and serving over capellini. In Pennsylvania, I can always create the flavor of this Italian recipe by finding good Sicilian olive oil and fresh, farm-grown eggplants at a nearby market. But I have great difficulty in imitating the particular blue of the Mediterranean sky.

3 medium eggplants, peeled and cut into ½-inch slices (you can choose to leave the skin on)
2 large sweet onions, cut into ½-inch slices
½ cup olive oil (I prefer to use a Sicilian olive oil for this recipe)
1 (28-ounce) can plum tomatoes, chopped, juice reserved
3 tablespoons capers, drained
½ cup pitted and sliced Kalamata olives
¼ cup balsamic vinegar
½ cup chopped fresh parsley
Salt and freshly ground black pepper

Preheat oven to 400°F.

Brush the eggplant and onion slices with olive oil and arrange on separate baking sheets.

Roast the eggplant and onion slices in the oven for 10 to 15 minutes, or until soft.

In a large saucepan, combine the tomatoes, capers, olives, and vinegar.

Cut the onion and eggplant slices into quarters and add them to the tomato mixture.

Toss well and season with salt and pepper to taste.

Add reserved juice if a thinner sauce is desired.

Sicilian Caponata tastes best if refrigerated for several hours or overnight, then reheated. It is good served over capellini and enjoyed with crusty Italian bread.

Cassis Crisp

Serves 12

A very, very dear friend of mine who was an adventuresome traveler and possessed a sophisticated approach to food took a cooking course one summer in France. She delighted in the experience as well as in what she had learned. Although my friend Barbara is no longer here to teach me about unique sources for fine decorating or fine food, or to give me advice daily, I am happy to possess one of the delicious recipes she brought back from Burgundy. Her original is copied on sheets of fax paper that are now pretty crumpled and include several annotations in her handwriting. Sometimes a recipe becomes very special because of the source.

The recipe begins with the French chef's words: "I've grown fond of gleaning creative cooking clues from the flavors professional wine tasters detect when describing Burgundy wines. Here, blueberries, raspberries, and strawberries go from hinted-at undertones in Côte de Nuits reds to Cassis-enriched reality in the most comforting of warm desserts. To give an essentially American-style fruit cobbler a bit more French flair, I have replaced the traditional crumbly nut-studded topping with a more sophisticated lemon-laced sugar-cookie crust. French vanilla ice cream, of course, would be a welcome and appropriate accompaniment."

Filling

2 pints blueberries
1½ pints raspberries
2 pints strawberries, hulled and quartered
½ cup granulated sugar
3 tablespoons unbleached all-purpose flour
⅓ cup Crème de Cassis

Cookie Crust

½ pound unsalted butter at room temperature
1 cup granulated sugar
1 egg
1 teaspoon vanilla extract
2 teaspoon grated lemon zest
1 cup unbleached all-purpose flour
Pinch of salt

Preheat oven to 375°F.

Mix all the berries with the sugar, flour, and Crème de Cassis; spread evenly in a 9 by 13-inch baking dish and set aside while making the cookie crust.

Cream the butter and sugar together (an electric mixer is fine to use) until smooth.

Beat in the egg, vanilla, and lemon zest.

Sift the flour, baking powder, and salt over the butter mixture.

With a wooden spoon, stir to incorporate the flour mixture and make a cookie-type batter.

Drop the topping over the berry mixture and spread evenly.

Bake for about 50 to 60 minutes, or until the top is light golden brown and the berry mixture is bubbling.

Let cool for 15 minutes before serving.

Best served warm, topped with French vanilla ice cream.

Arboretum Supporters Celebrate Spring

The inspiration for this celebratory dinner was easy when I combined my two great passions: the University of Pennsylvania's Morris Arboretum, and our contemporary craft dinnerware. In a tranquil setting at the Arboretum stands Toshiko Takaezu's beautiful bronze sculpture. Toshiko is a master potter and a recognized influential figure in ceramic art. Described as "blending Japanese tradition with Western aesthetics," Toshiko's wheel-thrown pots—as well as her large, exquisitely crafted sculptural forms—can be seen in numerous public installations, as well as in museums throughout the United States and Japan. A splendid setting was inevitable when I combined a collection of Toshiko's closed forms in the center of each table with balls of moss as placecard holders and glass cubes filled with white peonies.

In his London studio, glass artist Danny Lane created the wine goblets; the base remains on the table as you remove the stem to drink from the glass. The round service plates and unusually shaped dinner plates made by Israeli artist Samy D added interesting contours to the place settings, while the 24-karat-gold–rimmed soup bowls by Michael Wainwright, from Great Barrington, Massachusetts, added an elegant and timeless touch. Robyn Nichols, from Kansas City, Missouri, created the sterling-silver napkin rings, which added even more sparkle and a reference to the garden. Her entwined leaves boast "an insect bite" out of the metal. Dessert was presented on a ceramic plate by Dorothy Hafner. The iron-forged candlesticks are by Albert Paley, from Rochester, New York. I guess you could say it was an international gathering on top of the table.

Toshiko Takaezu bronze bell

Albert Paley iron-forged candlesticks, Toshiko Takaezu vessels

Samy D service and dinner plates

Robyn Nichols napkin ring

Michael Hurwitz plant stand

Danny Lane wine goblet

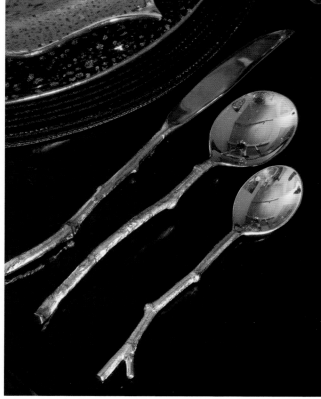

Michael Aram flatware

Parmesan Puffs

Makes approximately 40 puffs

This retro recipe seems to be enjoying a revival. It was very popular in the 1960s, and now I see it served at fancy parties by sophisticated catering services. I've always loved making this simple and delicious appetizer; the taste never gives away the ingredients.

1 cup grated Parmigiano–Reggiano cheese
½ cup mayonnaise
1 tablespoon minced onion
⅛ teaspoon cayenne (optional)
10 slices white sandwich bread, crusts removed

Preheat oven to 400°F.

Mix the cheese, mayonnaise, onion, and cayenne in a medium bowl and set aside.

Cut four circles from each slice of bread, using a cookie cutter or sharp knife (a shot glass also works well for cutting rounds).

Arrange rounds on a baking sheet and bake for 3 to 4 minutes, or until toasts are crisp and golden.

Cool toasts on baking sheet.

Top each toast round with ½ teaspoon of the cheese mixture, spreading it to the edge of the toasts.

Put the toasts back in the oven and bake for about 6 minutes, or until the tops are puffed and golden.

Remove from the oven and serve warm.

Cucumber-Dill Soup

Serves 12

4 cucumbers, peeled, seeded, and chopped
2 small onions, peeled and halved
8 cups plain yogurt
4 tablespoons fresh lime juice
2 tablespoons chopped chives
8 teaspoons olive oil
8 teaspoons white vinegar
4 teaspoons fresh dill, finely chopped
3 additional cups of finely chopped cucumber
3 teaspoons kosher salt
12 thin slices of unpeeled cucumber
12 sprigs fresh dill

In a blender, puree the four chopped cucumbers and onion and transfer to a bowl.

Add the yogurt, lime juice, chives, olive oil, and vinegar and mix well.

Add the finely chopped dill and cucumber.

Add salt.

Chill for at least one hour.

Garnish with additional slices of cucumber and a sprig of fresh dill.

Asparagus with Easy Hollandaise Sauce

Serves 12

4 pounds fresh asparagus
8 egg yolks
1 teaspoon salt
4 tablespoons fresh lemon juice
Dash of Tabasco sauce (optional)
1 pound butter, melted and slightly warm

Chop off the woody ends of the asparagus stalks. If the stalks are thick, peel the skin halfway down each stalk.

Place asparagus in a large pan of boiling salted water and blanch for about 10 minutes, or until tender. To keep the bright-green color, plunge the cooked asparagus into ice-cold water for just one or two seconds, and then remove the asparagus to a plate.

Meanwhile, place the egg yolks, salt, lemon juice, and Tabasco sauce in a blender and pulse the mixture well until thoroughly combined.

Slowly stream in the warm melted butter until the sauce comes together and emulsifies.

Arrange cooked asparagus on a serving plate.

Pour the hollandaise sauce over the warm asparagus and serve.

Herb-Tossed Potatoes

Serves 12

4 pounds small red-skin potatoes
8 tablespoons (1 stick) unsalted butter
3 teaspoons kosher salt
1 teaspoon freshly ground black pepper
6 tablespoons of green herbs: dill, parsley, chives,
and rosemary combined

With a small potato peeler, remove a circle of skin around the middle of each potato.

Melt the butter in a heavy skillet.

Add the potatoes, salt, and pepper and toss.

Cover and cook over low heat for about 25 minutes, stirring occasionally, until the potatoes are tender.

Toss the herbs with the potatoes and serve while hot.

The potatoes can be made ahead of serving time and reheated.

Rack of Lamb

Serves 12

6 tablespoons olive oil
3 large shallots, chopped
¾ cup balsamic vinegar
6 cups fresh bread crumbs
6 tablespoons finely chopped fresh thyme
6 frenched racks of lamb (8 ribs in each rack yields a total of 48 chops and serves each person 2 double chops)
4 tablespoons Dijon mustard
Salt and freshly ground black pepper

Preheat oven to 450°F.

In a sauté pan, heat the olive oil over moderate heat.

Add the chopped shallots and sauté until they are golden, stirring often.

Lower the heat and add the balsamic vinegar. Simmer for about 5 minutes.

Remove the pan from the heat and stir in the bread crumbs and thyme. Set aside.

Arrange the racks of lamb in a roasting pan, rib sides down.

Paint the meaty sides of the lamb with the Dijon mustard.

Season with salt and pepper.

Pat the bread-crumb mixture onto each rack, pressing the mixture into the mustard.

Roast the racks at 450°F for 10 minutes, then lower the heat to 400°F and continue to cook for another 15 to 20 minutes, or until the internal temperature of 130°F is reached for rare meat and 145° for medium.

Remove the lamb from the oven and cover the racks loosely with aluminum foil and a towel over the foil for 10 minutes. While covered, the lamb will continue to cook for a few more minutes and the juices will relax through the meat, making it easier to cut.

At serving time, place the cooked racks on a cutting board, slice each rack in half, and slice each half in half again. From each rack, there should be four double-ribbed pieces of lamb with two rib bones in each piece.

The crust may fall off during carving; simply press it back onto the chops before serving.

Arrange the lamb chops by interlocking the bones attractively, and serve.

Briques de Neige

Each loaf serves 12

My friend and great cook Kit Cornell writes, "I thank Abby Mandel, who created this decadent confection. I altered the recipe to produce two loaves and call it Briques de Neige—*one for immediate serving and one to freeze for later use. However, the presentation is more attractive when made in a bowl. I offer the loaf version as an alternative."* Pictured (opposite) is Kit's Boule de Neige.

4 cups semisweet chocolate chips
1½ cups hot, strong decaffeinated coffee
3 cups sugar
6 sticks unsalted butter at room temperature
14 eggs, beaten
3 tablespoons rum, brandy, or chocolate liqueur (optional)
Whipped cream to decorate

Preheat oven to 350°F.

Line two 9½ by 5½ by 2½-inch loaf pans with aluminum foil, pressing the foil into the corners and being careful not to tear it.

Melt the chocolate chips, coffee, and sugar together in a large heavy saucepan over low heat, being very careful not to burn the chocolate.

Using a hand mixer, carefully beat the mixture on low speed until the melted ingredients are thoroughly combined.

Add the butter, a few pieces at a time, and continue beating after each addition until all the butter is incorporated into the chocolate mixture.

Add the liqueur and beat on low speed until well mixed.

Remove the saucepan from the heat and pour the mixture into the prepared loaf pans. Place the loaf pans in a large, deep pan, and fill the large pan with boiling water until the water reaches halfway up the sides of the loaf pans. (The water keeps the briques de neige soft and moist during baking.)

Bake at 350°F for 1 hour, or until done.

Note: The cake will rise above the sides of the loaf pans while baking. When the tops appear crusty and can be jiggled without showing any liquid underneath, the loaves are done. The insides will still be "wet" if tested with a cake tester. The cakes will firm up when placed in the refrigerator to cool.

Remove the loaves from the oven and from the water bath and place them on a cooling rack.

Weight down both loaves until they are cool. I use a wooden cutting board to cover the loaf pans and then place additional weight (cans of soup or a brick will work, if you have one handy) on top of the board. Remove the board and weights and refrigerate the loaves in the pans overnight.

After the loaves have chilled completely, you can wrap one (or both) with plastic wrap and aluminum foil and freeze it for later use.

When the loaves are thoroughly chilled, flip the pans over to remove the briques de neige and peel the foil off the cakes. It is unfair to call them cake because the consistency is denser than a cake and more like a mousse or chocolate pâté.

Cover each brique de neige with fresh whipped cream in any attractive way you choose.

Dorothy Hafner plate

Tea Party in the Garden

One of my most memorable cooking days in the kitchen was when I invited my granddaughters to make and decorate cupcakes. Of course, after all the fun we had decorating, we had to enjoy them ourselves. What better way then to have a tea party—hats and all?

To decorate the cupcakes, I gathered a variety of colored glitter sugars, sprinkles of every shape, edible decorations, fresh fruit, and cake-decorating icing tubes. The frosting—out of a store-bought can—was a simple and perfect choice. I put each decorating selection in a different dish, and when the cupcakes cooled, the girls—with their own ideas about decorating—set to creative work. I was amazed at the results; the cupcakes looked like they came straight from a fancy bakery! The girls were amazed at how good the all-time favorite chocolate-brownie cupcakes tasted.

The pavilion in the garden, designed by the architect and designer Michael Graves, was the ideal place to hold a tea party. We set the table with a pink-and-white-striped cotton cloth and then used vintage white gloves, which I had once gathered for a similar setting, underneath Roberta Bloom's white porcelain plates and cups and saucers. Karen Aumann's pitcher—with a whimsical design of garden leeks that reflects English Victorian ware—held daisies. The pitcher for the cream and tea cup holding sugar were made by Maryland potter Liz Langsfeld. A sculpture by Gina Rose Halpern provided a whimsical centerpiece for our garden setting.

We left our cell phones behind, and over tea, while wearing hats and our "jewels," the respite from technology gave way to conversation and giggles centered on how to hold your pinkie finger properly when drinking from a teacup.

Roberta Bloom plates, cups, and saucers
Karen Aumann pitcher
Gina Rose Halpern sculpture
Collection of vintage gloves

Liz Langsfeld teacup and pitcher
Roberta Bloom plate, cup, and saucer

Tea Sandwiches

These little sandwiches are everyone's favorite for lunch or tea and are so quickly consumed that no matter how many you make, there are never any leftovers. It is important that they look pretty, as well as taste great. Although there are many good sources for ready-made tea sandwiches, these are very easy to make.

Remove the crusts from a variety of thinly sliced soft breads, such as white, whole wheat, and pumpernickel.

Stack a few slices on top of each other and flatten the stack with a rolling pin.

Peel the slices apart; cut shapes with a cookie cutter or a sharp knife into rounds, fingers, or triangles; and spread softened sweet butter on each slice.

Spread your favorite fillings evenly over the slices and top with remaining bread slices.

We love the traditional minced tuna salad, deviled eggs with watercress, steamed asparagus rolled in white bread, smoked salmon with dill butter, and cream cheese and chutney, just to mention a few.

Chocolate-Brownie Cupcakes

Makes 12

1 cup all-purpose flour
1 teaspoon baking powder
1 teaspoon salt
6 tablespoons unsalted butter
6 ounces dark chocolate, chopped
¾ cup sugar
2 eggs
1 teaspoon pure vanilla extract

Preheat oven to 350°F.

Mix flour, baking powder, and salt together in a bowl.

Put butter, chocolate, and sugar in the top of a double boiler and heat over boiling water, while stirring the ingredients, until the butter and chocolate are melted.

Remove from heat.

Add the eggs, one at a time, to the melted chocolate, beating the mixture after each addition.

Add the vanilla extract.

Add the dry ingredients a little at a time and mix until combined to make a batter.

Line 12 cups in a muffin or cupcake pan with paper liners.

Spoon batter into the 12 cups, filling each approximately three-quarters full.

Bake for 20 to 25 minutes, or until the cupcakes form a light crust on the top but are still soft on the inside.

Cool the cupcakes completely before removing them from the pan.

Decorate the cupcakes with your favorite frosting and toppings.

Craft Show Luncheon

The Philadelphia Museum of Art Craft Show is presented annually by the museum's Women's Committee and Craft Show Committee to benefit the museum. Each year, the committees gather at a member's home to personalize invitations to the show, which is held in the fall. While addressing the envelopes and affixing stamps, the conversation around the table is lively and often includes the exchange of summer travel plans, learning about children's achievements in the past year, and, of course, sharing glowing reports of grandchildren. Lunch is almost secondary to the good time we all enjoy. I am always happy when it is my turn to host the event.

Peter Olster orchestrated his excellent team from Philadelphia's Betty the Caterer to prepare a delicious buffet, with great respect for the tableware I wanted to use.

Morning coffee was set out with cups and saucers by Pennsylvania ceramist Lisa Naples, who adapts simple motifs from nature in her functional ware. The curl of a saucer rim or the bend of a cup's handle imitates familiar branches or leaves in her designs. The carved porcelain creamer and sugar bowl with yellow glazed interiors were made by Elizabeth Lurie.

After a couple of hours of diligent attention to the invitations, lunch was served from a buffet in the kitchen, using Claudia Reese's colorful plates. The salmon was sliced and served on a long tray made by Jack Charney. No two of Jack's platters are alike; his colorful painting is unique to each piece. The watermelon salad was served from a brightly glazed bowl made by Israeli artist Vered Tandler Dayan, with the red glaze accenting the red of the watermelon and the radishes.

Forks were rolled in dish towels that were used as napkins, and lemonade or iced tea was served in Mason jar mugs that Peter brought. The jars were perfect to carry to a table outside, where everyone enjoyed a beautiful day. Chocolate Chocolate-Chip cookies were served from farm-market baskets.

Lisa Naples cups and saucers
Elizabeth Lurie creamer and sugar

Claudia Reese plates

Vered Tandler Dayan bowl

Farm-Market Vegetable Salad

Serves 12

3 cups watercress, tough stems removed and leaves cut into small pieces
3 cups baby arugula leaves
4 cups diced celery or fennel bulb
1 cup chopped red onion
4 cups cherry tomatoes, halved
4 cups sliced radishes
1 pound string beans, trimmed and steamed
1 small avocado, peeled and cubed
6 tablespoons fresh lemon juice
6 tablespoons fresh orange juice
6 tablespoons fresh lime juice
6 teaspoons sugar
6 teaspoons extra-virgin olive oil
6 tablespoons minced fresh mint leaves
Salt and freshly ground black pepper

Combine watercress, arugula, celery or fennel, onion, tomatoes, radishes, beans, and avocado in a large bowl.

In a small bowl, whisk lemon, orange, and lime juices; sugar; and olive oil. Stir in mint.

Add salt and pepper to taste.

Pour the dressing over the vegetables, tossing gently to coat.

Serve the vegetables alone or on salad greens.

Watermelon, Feta, and Radish Salad

Serves 12

A Craft Show Committee member requested this delightful salad, having enjoyed it several years ago at a similar gathering at my home. The crunch of the radishes adds to the taste of this salad as well as to its visual appearance. How good does a request to repeat a recipe make you feel?!

Vinaigrette

¼ cup fresh lemon juice
¼ cup orange juice
¼ cup chopped shallots
1 tablespoon honey
1 teaspoon salt
1 teaspoon freshly ground black pepper
½ cup olive oil

Whisk together all the ingredients to make the vinaigrette.

Salad

6 cups cubed and seeded watermelon
2 cups crumbled feta cheese
1½ cups sliced radishes
½ cup chopped fresh mint leaves
1 cup sliced pitted black olives

Toss the watermelon with the feta, radishes, mint leaves, and black olives and add the vinaigrette, a little at a time, until you reach the desired flavor.

This salad should not be soggy.

Salmon en Croûte

Serves 12

1 tablespoon pickled ginger
2 cups water
2 cups white wine
2 cups soy sauce
1 (3- to 4-pound) boneless, skinless fillet of salmon
8 ounces vegetable oil
4 large shallots, sliced
16 portobello mushroom caps, gills removed and caps cut into a ¾-inch dice
Salt and freshly ground black pepper
2 cups fresh spinach
1 (12-ounce) puff-pastry sheet, approximately 10 by 15 inches, thawed
2 eggs beaten with a bit of water, for the egg wash

Combine the ginger, water, wine, and soy sauce in a large pan or dish.

Cut a 1-inch deep incision lengthwise along the salmon fillet.

Place the salmon in the soy-sauce mixture and marinate for at least 3 hours.

Preheat oven to 400°F.

In a large sauté pan, warm 4 ounces of the vegetable oil over moderate heat.

Add the shallots and cook until translucent, approximately 2 to 3 minutes.

Add the mushrooms and season with salt and pepper.

Cook until the mushrooms are tender, remove from heat, place the mixture in a bowl, and set aside.

Into the same sauté pan, add the remainder of the vegetable oil.

Wilt the spinach slightly in the oil over medium heat.

Season with salt and pepper.

Remove the salmon fillet from the marinade and pat dry.

Fill the salmon cavity with the mushroom-shallot mixture.

Place half of the wilted spinach on top of the mushrooms.

Lay the puff-pastry sheet on a lightly floured surface.

Spread the other half of the spinach on the bottom third of the pastry.

Carefully lay the salmon, cut side down, on the spinach, and wrap the pastry sheet around the salmon.

Brush the pastry with the egg wash.

Place the salmon on a sheet pan or in a baking dish and bake for approximately 35 minutes, or until the pastry is golden brown and the internal temperature is 140°F.

Peter Olster prepared this to be served at room temperature as a perfect luncheon dish.

Jack Charney platter

Chocolate Chocolate-Chip Cookies

Makes 24 cookies

I have a reputation for being a chocolate addict. I guess I am guilty because I never feel as though it's a dessert unless it includes chocolate. I even love a chocolate-chip cookie that boasts double the chocolate, as in this recipe adapted from Ghirardelli Chocolate.

1 (11.5-ounce) bag bittersweet chocolate chips
6 tablespoons unsalted butter
3 eggs
1 cup sugar
⅓ cup all-purpose flour
½ teaspoon baking powder
1 (11.5-ounce) bag semisweet chocolate chips
1 cup chopped walnuts

In a double boiler over hot water, melt the bittersweet chocolate chips and butter.

In a large bowl, beat the eggs and sugar with an electric mixer until thickened.

Slowly stir in the chocolate mixture.

In a small bowl, mix together the flour and baking powder and add the flour mixture, a little at a time, to the chocolate mixture.

Gently fold in the semisweet chocolate chips and walnuts.

Form two logs with the dough and wrap them tightly with plastic wrap. (The dough will be very soft.)

Refrigerate for at least 1 hour, or until firm.

Preheat oven to 375°F.

Grease two cookie sheets or line them with parchment paper.

Unwrap the dough, and with a sharp knife, cut the logs into ¾-inch slices.

Place the slices 1½ inches apart on the prepared cookie sheets.

Bake for 12 to 14 minutes, or until a shiny crust forms on the tops of the cookies and the interiors are still soft.

Claude and Francois-Xavier Lalanne bronze sheep

Good Friends, Good Recipes:
Wendell Castle and Nancy Jurs's Chocolate Chestnut Parnham

Wendell Castle and I became good friends years ago when we both served on the American Craft Council's board of directors. Since the board was made up of members from all over the country who had to make their way to New York City, the meeting was held over two days. During one rather lengthy meeting, I passed a note to Wendell to tell him that I was thinking of a new dining-room table and to ask whether he would be interested in designing and making one for me. He made a few quick sketches and passed the note back, saying he would be delighted. I sent the note back to him, indicating the sketches I particularly loved, and he sent the note back to me with his refined ideas for the design.

That exchange initiated a wonderful commission for a long dining-room table that seats sixteen people and which can also be separated into two square tables. The incredible design includes a bronze base with ball-bearing wheels that make moving the two-part table quite simple.

After living with Wendell's beautifully designed table, which is made of Imbuya wood with satinwood inlays, I realized that my dining chairs didn't work with his design, so I decided that the table should have Wendell Castle chairs around it.

At another Council board meeting, I again passed a note to Wendell to tell him that I was thinking about dining chairs. His reply, passed back on a note, said simply, "I was hoping you would say that."

Wendell and his wife Nancy's recipe once won first prize at a bake-off fund-raising event in Rochester, New York.

Serves 10 to 12

½ pound semisweet or sweet chocolate
6 ounces unsalted butter
6 ounces icing sugar, sifted
1 (1-pound) can chestnut puree
Juice of 1 small orange
1 teaspoon grated orange rind
2 tablespoons Grand Marnier
½ pint heavy cream, whipped to soft peaks

Lightly grease a spring-form pan with butter.

Melt the chocolate in a double boiler over hot water.

Beat the butter with the sugar until fluffy.

Stir in the melted chocolate.

Add the chestnut puree to the chocolate mixture.

Add the orange juice, grated orange rind, and Grand Marnier.

Pour the mixture into the pan and chill several hours.

To remove it from the pan, run a knife around the inside edge of the pan and invert onto a serving plate.

Top each portion with whipped cream and a touch of shaved chocolate and serve.

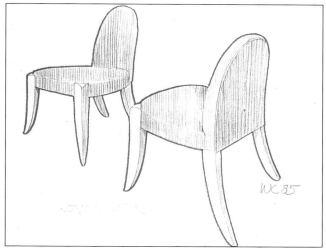

Wendell Castle table base and chairs (detail)

Summer By the Ocean

In late summer 1986, while helping our youngest daughter move into her college dormitory, Leonard and I received a phone call that informed us that a property in New Jersey we had been interested in was ours. To mark the occasion, we bought a poster announcing that year's America's Cup sailing regatta, and it still hangs in our house today.

The thought of building a family retreat at the beach was exciting, and since then, Margate, New Jersey, has always been a special place for us. When we leave the Pennsylvania countryside and head to the shore, the first thing we always do when we cross over the bridge above the bay is open the car windows so that we can feel the breeze and smell the saltiness of the ocean, knowing its great roar will greet us in a moment. The calm feeling that we instantly sense when we cross the bridge into town lasts the entire time we remain at our beach house.

Today, we have enjoyed over two decades of easy summer living in the house we built and named CASUAL 111 after our daughters CAthy, SUzy, and ALison. The address of the house is 111. To keep track of all the things we would need for our new house during the process of getting acquainted with it, we enlisted the help of our friend Kit Finley Cornell, who would ultimately spend many summers managing the house and what needed to be done to it during the week while also preparing delicious meals on weekends. CASUAL 111 is a place for family gatherings and summer parties. Beginning Memorial Day weekend and ending after Labor Day, long weekends at CASUAL 111 have become a welcome ritual.

Together, Kit and I have pored over recipes. We experimented in the kitchen, laughed over some of our catastrophes—accidents that were mostly a result of my being overly ambitious—and beamed with delight when we came up with a new recipe. One of us would often exclaim, "Save that recipe for the cookbook!" For twenty years, thanks to Kit's detailed record keeping and her desire to document each summer's parties, we have collected numerous recipes and summer entertaining plans.

Among our dear friends, we are fortunate to count several couples whose friendship has continued since high school days. With them, we have celebrated marriages, the birth of children, and can now proudly revel in our grandchildren. Every summer for the past twenty years, we have gathered with our friends for an annual house-party weekend. The days are very relaxed and center around lots of reading on the deck, long walks on the beach, and, of course, a well-stocked refrigerator for self-serve snacks. Dinner is usually planned for tables on the deck unless the ocean breeze is too strong, in which case we hear the roar of the ocean from inside, through screened doors.

Everyone who stays at our home knows that one drawer in the kitchen always contains a box of chocolates from the local chocolate maker—the ultimate snack, or a fine conclusion to any dinner.

Summer Menus

"The first summer I spent at CASUAL 111 was the beginning of a lasting friendship with Jane, Lenny, and their children, and the beginning of many summers of good food, happy houseguests, family gatherings, and memorable parties.

We always had local fruits and vegetables on hand and a tin of homemade pita chips. Summer after summer, weekends were always relaxed, and I got to know the guests and to anticipate their favorite foods and the way they liked their coffee. I recorded every event so that we could go back to the menus from previous years and prepare only the houseguests' favorites. The Kormans' friends have become my friends."

—Kit Cornell

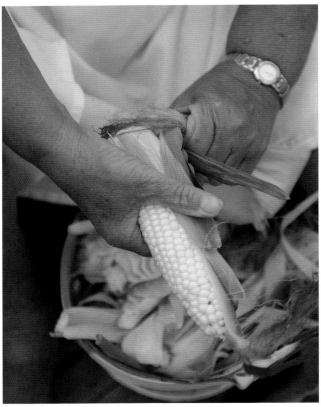

Friday Night—The Gang's All Here

CASUAL 111 is a place for family gatherings as well as for a twenty-year tradition, our annual house-party weekend we share with many dear friends. The "gang" arrives late Friday afternoon for a weekend of relaxation, walks on the beach, and good food and conversation.

The napkins were made at the Fabric Workshop and Museum in Philadelphia from *Maze,* a pattern designed by Edna Andrade in 1984. The Fabric Workshop and Museum invites artists working in various media to serve as artists-in-residence and experience the art of printing on fabric. A collection of Van Briggle vases from Colorado Springs held lady's mantle and white rugosa roses. Over the years, I collected the pottery from flea markets and antique stores. The rich glazes remind me of soft-looking marble; they are as attractive displayed by themselves on shelves as they are functional on the table.

The chargers were made by Yoshiaki Yuki, a Japanese artist whose calligraphy-inspired designs are used on his ceramic tableware. Translating for Mr. Yuki, Timothy Di Fiore, the managing director of Gallery Gen in New York City, said, "No matter how beautiful a clay pot is, it should be touched and used every day."

The wine glasses were designed by Michelle Ivankovic. She recycles thrift-shop glasses by sandblasting them, creating a unity among the mismatched shapes. I enjoy the way they feel and the fact that they are so eco-friendly.

The water goblets are from La Verrerie de Biot in the south of France, where, after we had watched the master glassblowers at their foundry, we had the pleasure of selecting the finished glasses. Although the glasses look delicate on the table, they have thick stems, so they easily survived shipping overseas.

Hummus was served in vintage teacups with handblown stems, which I purchased at the gift shop at the Victoria and Albert Museum in London.

Its fine steel blade set in a beautifully carved wooden handle, the knife used to slice the baked salami was made by Joseph DiGangi. The beauty of the design of these patented knives, along with their perfect balance, makes them ideal for cutting and exquisite to use for serving. The baked salami was served on a Kohiki platter designed by Japanese-born artist Akira Satake.

The gazpacho was served in handblown Windsor tankards by Simon Pearce in Vermont. There is nothing better than clear glass to show off a beautiful color.

The dessert plates are by Marek Cecula, whose work overlaps art and industrial design, and whose passion for the use of ceramics in both fields leads him on many paths, including one as an educator.

Fabric Workshop and Museum napkins
A collection of Van Briggle pottery
Yoshiaki Yuki chargers
Michelle Ivankovic Frosine goblets
La Verrerie de Biot water goblets

Vintage teacups with handblown stems

Simon Pearce glass tankards

Homemade Hummus with Pita Chips

Serves 6 to 8

Hummus

¼ cup vegetable oil
¼ cup lemon juice
1 garlic clove, minced
Pinch of salt and freshly ground black pepper
1 (15-ounce) can chickpeas, drained and rinsed
Handful of fresh parsley, chopped

In a food processor, blend the oil, lemon juice, garlic, salt, and pepper until smooth.

Add chickpeas a little at a time and continue to process until the mixture is smooth.

Toss in chopped parsley and process until combined.

If you prefer a thinner hummus, add more oil, a tablespoon at a time, until the hummus is the consistency you like.

Pita Chips

6 pita pockets, each sliced into 8 wedges
¼ pound (1 stick) salted butter, melted

Preheat oven to 350°F.

Separate the top halves from the bottom halves of each pita wedge; you should have 16 triangles.

Using a pastry brush, paint each triangle with the melted butter.

Assemble the triangles on a baking sheet and bake for a few minutes until the chips are golden brown and crisp. The chips will continue to bake after they are removed from the oven, so pull them out just short of the golden color you desire.

Cool completely.

Serve with hummus or your favorite dip.

For extra flavor, try sprinkling fresh or dried herbs on the chips before baking them. Keep your eye on them while they bake; the herbs can burn quickly. Chips will keep for about two weeks if stored in an airtight container.

Baked Salami

Serves 6 to 8

This is such a delicious and easy-to-prepare appetizer that it will surprise and please even the most sophisticated eater.

1 (2-pound) kosher salami (we use Hebrew National)
1 cup of your favorite barbecue sauce

Preheat oven to 325°F.

Line a baking sheet with aluminum foil.

Peel the wrapping off the salami.

Cut a thin strip lengthwise along one side of the salami so it doesn't roll on the baking sheet.

Score the top of the salami, making ¼-inch-deep X-shaped cuts.

Place the salami flat side down on the baking sheet.

Brush the salami with 1/2 cup barbecue sauce (a pastry brush works well for this).

Bake for 20 minutes.

Brush the remaining barbecue sauce on the salami and bake for another 15 minutes, until the salami is browned. Allow the salami to cool for several minutes before serving.

As an accompaniment, serve black bread slices cut in triangles.

Joseph DiGangi knife, Akira Satake platter

Golden Gazpacho*

Serves 6 to 8

This soup tastes best in the summer, when local yellow heirloom tomatoes are available. It's also great the next day and can be garnished with chopped cucumbers or lump crabmeat.

½ cup chopped sweet onion
1 clove garlic, peeled
5 yellow tomatoes, cored and coarsely chopped
5 yellow peppers, cored and coarsely chopped
1 cucumber, peeled, seeded, and coarsely chopped
8 whole almonds
½ cup olive oil
4 tablespoons white balsamic vinegar
1 tablespoon plain bread crumbs
3 tablespoons fresh or bottled lime juice
2 teaspoons kosher salt
½ teaspoon coarsely ground black pepper
1 tablespoon chopped chives
½ tablespoon minced parsley

Simon Pearce glass tankard

In a blender or food processor, pulse onions, garlic, tomatoes, peppers, cucumber, and almonds until they are lightly combined. Work in batches; the soup should be on the chunky side.

Pour the vegetable mixture into a large bowl.

Stir the remaining ingredients into the vegetable mixture.

Cover and refrigerate for at least 4 hours before serving.

Check seasoning and add additional salt and pepper to taste.

*Adapted from Feast Your Eyes Catering in Philadelphia

Crispy Fried Chicken

Serves 6 to 8

2 (3-pound) whole chickens, cut into 8 pieces each
    (2 wings, 2 breasts, 2 thighs, and 2 drumsticks)
1 quart buttermilk
2 cups all-purpose flour
1 tablespoon salt
1 tablespoon freshly ground black pepper
6 eggs, beaten
3 cups (or more, if necessary) Crisco or other
    solid vegetable shortening

Place the chicken in a large glass or nonreactive baking dish and pour the buttermilk over it, making sure all pieces are covered.

Cover and refrigerate for at least 3 hours, or overnight.

Remove the chicken from the buttermilk and pat dry with a paper towel.

Place the flour, salt, and pepper in a medium-size bowl and mix.

Dredge each chicken piece in the seasoned flour and shake off the excess flour.

Dip each piece of chicken in the beaten eggs and then dredge in the flour mixture again.

Let the chicken rest for a few minutes.

Heat the Crisco or shortening to 350°F in an electric frying pan or large heavy skillet. The melted shortening should be deep enough to allow the chicken to float.

Place chicken, a few pieces at a time, in the hot oil, being careful not to overcrowd the pieces. Do not let the oil bubble over.

Cook the pieces until they are golden on one side, then flip pieces and cook until the other side is golden. Sometimes I turn my chicken more than once if it's browning too quickly. Make certain to maintain the 350°F temperature of the oil so that the chicken cooks completely.

Each bone-in piece should take about 18 minutes to cook. Add a few more minutes to the cooking time for exceptionally large pieces.

Remove chicken pieces and drain on a baking sheet lined with the unprinted side of a brown-paper grocery bag, topped with a layer of paper towels.

Change the paper linings of the baking sheet as they become saturated with oil.

To reheat the chicken, place the pieces on a clean baking sheet lined with a brown-paper grocery bag, printed side down and without the paper-towel lining, and warm gently in a 325°F oven.

Tomatoes 111

Serves 6 to 8

This is an adaptation of a recipe that is served at a local restaurant. It is best made in July and August, when the Jersey tomatoes are at their peak. The drained, cooled shallots can be stored in an airtight container lined with aluminum foil until you are ready to use them. If you cannot find sherry vinegar, you can make a classic vinaigrette with cider vinegar. A rice-vinegar dressing is delicious too.

3 or 4 medium-ripe tomatoes, sliced into ½-inch-thick slices
⅓ cup sherry vinegar
½ teaspoon prepared Dijon mustard
½ cup olive oil
1 cup flour, for dredging shallots
½ teaspoon each salt and freshly ground black pepper
3 large shallots, sliced thin lengthwise
1 egg, beaten
1 cup Crisco
½ cup (or more) crumbled Roquefort cheese
8 fresh basil leaves
1 large sprig of fresh basil, for garnish

Arrange tomato slices on a serving platter and set aside.

Whisk the sherry vinegar and mustard together.

Add the olive oil in a steady stream as you continue to whisk until the vinaigrette is the consistency you prefer. The longer you whisk, the thicker the dressing will become.

Add salt and freshly ground pepper to the vinaigrette to taste. Set the vinaigrette aside.

Place the flour, salt, and pepper in a medium bowl.

Dip the shallots into the egg, dredge them in the seasoned flour, and shake off the excess flour.

Heat the Crisco to 350°F in a heavy skillet and fry the shallots in it until they are crisp and golden.

Drain the shallots on paper towels.

Drizzle the vinaigrette over the assembled tomato slices.

Sprinkle the crumbled Roquefort on the tomatoes and the crispy shallots on top of the cheese.

Immediately before serving, snip the fresh basil into pieces and sprinkle it over the entire dish. Garnish with the large sprig of basil to complete the look.

In the photograph above, the tomatoes on the kitchen counter sit in front of a collection of Cornish kitchenware that I gathered piece by piece from flea markets and antique shops.

Kit's Corn Bread

Serves 6 to 8

This is a very moist corn bread, so if you're used to the crumbly, dry style, you're in for a treat.

2 (8.5-ounce) boxes of corn-muffin mix (I prefer Jiffy)
1 (14.5-ounce) can of cream-style corn
1 (16-ounce) container sour cream (low-fat is OK but not no-fat)
1 cup corn oil
2 pinches of salt
6 eggs, lightly beaten

Preheat oven to 375°F.

Spray a 9 by 13-inch baking dish with cooking spray and line it with parchment paper.

Empty the muffin mixes into a large bowl.

In another bowl, mix the corn, sour cream, oil, and salt.

Combine the beaten eggs with the corn mixture and pour it all into the muffin mix.

Stir well to evenly blend all ingredients.

Pour into the prepared baking dish and bake for 55 minutes, or until deep golden brown.

The top should feel firm when you touch it.

Cool the corn bread on a rack before cutting.

Peach Shortcakes

Serves 6 to 8

If the peaches are very sweet and juicy, you don't need to add sugar to them. However, sprinkling some granulated sugar over them will create some natural juices that are delicious when drizzled over the bottom shortcake before you build your dessert. To keep the cut peaches from discoloring because of oxidation, cover them with plastic wrap placed directly over them, and seal the wrap around the edges to keep the air out. If this is done properly, the peaches will look freshly cut for up to 24 hours.

2⅓ cups Bisquick Original baking mix
½ cup milk
3 tablespoons sugar
3 tablespoons butter, melted
1½ tablespoons powdered cinnamon and 1½ tablespoons granulated sugar, mixed
9 fresh peaches, blanched for one minute, peeled, pitted, and each sliced into wedges
Granulated sugar (optional)
1½ cups heavy cream
1 teaspoon 10X confectioners' sugar
Fresh raspberries and mint leaves, for garnish

Preheat oven to 425°F.

In a large bowl, stir together the Bisquick mix, milk, sugar and melted butter until the mixture forms into a soft dough.

Divide the dough into 6 portions and place each portion on an ungreased baking sheet.

Sprinkle each portion with the cinnamon and sugar mixture.

Bake for 10 to 12 minutes, until golden brown.

Let the shortcakes cool slightly and then split them in half horizontally while they are still warm, using a serrated knife.

To make the whipped cream, chill electric-mixer beaters and a large metal bowl. Beat the heavy cream and confectioners' sugar together in the bowl until the mixture reaches the desired consistency. (I like a soft whipped cream on top of the assembled shortcake.)

To assemble the servings, place the bottom half of each shortcake on a plate. Mound the fresh peaches on the shortcake, place a dollop of freshly whipped cream on the top, and top it with the other half of the shortcake. Garnish with the berries and mint.

Marek Cecula plate

Saturday Night on the Deck

It's Saturday night, and neighbors and friends join us and our weekend house guests for dinner. Sometimes we ask everyone to help with the preparations, cooking, or tend the barbeque. It is a night when we all participate in making a meal, and the process produces a lot of laughs (and sometimes a little anxiety).

One very special dish is Dr. David Paskin's Fried Mozzarella with Marinara Sauce, which was created by a dear friend who has enjoyed a lifetime of fame and glory. The fame came from the operating room at Pennsylvania Hospital, where, as a surgeon, he saved many lives, and the glory comes from his expert hands in the kitchen when he cooks for special friends. Our kitchen in the beach house is equipped with electric burners, which make it slightly difficult to get the oil hot enough to fry the mozzarella. This can create stressful moments as we hover over the pot and wait for it to boil. Cheers arise when the first bubbles are spotted.

The tables on the deck were set with custom-made cloths from Philadelphia's JRB Linens, where Judy Block specializes in finding the right fabric to custom make linens for any size table and any setting. I chose blue-and-white seersucker cloths and ruffle-edged yellow-and-white seersucker napkins because they were a wonderful background for the same colors of the hand-thrown pottery by Alec Karros. The dinner plates, dessert plates, and oversized wine goblets made a bright setting.

As centerpieces, I used vintage sand pails, collected over the years from area flea markets, that I filled with flowers—chrysanthemums, bright zinnias, or marigolds—from our garden. The whole combination said, "Summer is here."

JRB Linens tablecloth and napkins
Alec Karros wine goblets, dinner plates, and dessert plates
Vintage sand pail

Barbara Eigen pitcher

Vintage sand pails

Pimm's Cup

For each individual serving

While visiting friends outside London several years ago, our two teenage grandchildren were introduced to the very British drink Pimm's Cup. I don't know what delighted the teenagers the most: the fact that it is respectable in England to join the adults in a drink before dinner or the actual delicious drink itself. We reviewed the trip when we returned home; the highlight that our grandchildren always remembered was not Royal Ascot and seeing the queen in her royal carriage, or taking pictures with the beefeaters at the Tower of London, but the introduction to Pimm's.

2 fluid ounces (120-ml) Pimm's No. 1
½ cup (4 fluid ounces) ginger ale, 7UP, or lemon-lime soda
Slice of lemon
Slice of cucumber, for garnish

Pour the Pimm's and ginger ale, 7UP, or lemon-lime soda into a chilled glass over ice.

Squeeze the lemon slice as you drop it into the glass.

Stir gently.

Garnish with the cucumber slice.

Gravlax

Serves 12 to 14

Gravlax is fresh salmon cured in a Scandinavian way, and I love to serve it any time of year. Although it is very simple to make, it requires a couple of days in the refrigerator while the salmon marinates and you turn it in the brine that is created by the salt and sugar. A board and heavy weights need to be placed on top of the salmon to ensure the curing process. When I use my 5-pound free weights for this, people who open the refrigerator door never cease to offer a few comments, if not smiles. A heavy frying pan or pot will do the same trick, and there is no difference in the taste of the gravlax.

½ **cup granulated sugar**
½ **cup kosher salt**
2 teaspoons coarsely ground black pepper
1 teaspoon dried thyme
1 teaspoon dried dill
1 large bunch fresh dill
1 (3-pound) boned fillet of salmon, skin left on

Combine sugar, salt, pepper, thyme, and dried dill in a small bowl and mix well.

Sprinkle the spice mixture on both sides of the salmon.

Cut the salmon in half lengthwise (or you can have your fishmonger do this for you at the store).

Place one piece of the salmon, skin side down, in a shallow glass dish, and top the piece with the fresh dill, reserving some for garnish.

Place the other piece of salmon, skin side up, directly on top of the first.

Cover the salmon tightly with foil or plastic wrap.

Place a flat dish or cutting board on top of the fish.

Place a frying pan on top of the board and weight it down with heavy cans or something comparable.

Refrigerate the salmon for 36 to 48 hours, turning the fish over every 12 hours and spooning the juices that collect in the dish over the fish, then rewrapping it.

To serve the salmon, lay it on a cutting board and scrape off most of the fresh dill and spices.

With a sharp knife, carefully cut the salmon into thin slices and place the slices on a serving platter.

Garnish with the remaining fresh dill and serve with black bread.

Dr. David's Fried Mozzarella with Marinara Sauce

Serves 6 to 8

Fried Mozzarella

18 eggs
2 (16-ounce) packages part-skim mozzarella cheese
1½ (15-ounce) cans plain bread crumbs
4 quarts canola oil

Beat 6 eggs in a bowl.

Pour one-third of the bread crumbs onto a plate.

Cut the ends of each block of cheese so that the cheese is squared off into a block, and then cut each block into 4 slices.

Dip one slice of cheese in the beaten egg and then into the bread crumbs, coating each side. Set the coated slice aside on a clean plate.

Continue this method until all 8 slices are coated.

Discard the used eggs and bread crumbs.

Beat 6 more eggs and put another third of the bread crumbs onto a plate; dip the coated cheese slices in the egg and then into the bread crumbs, again coating each side.

Repeat, discarding the used eggs and bread crumbs after each coating. A total of three coatings will produce a thick shell around the cheese.

Let the breaded cheese sit for 1 hour.

Pour the oil into a large pot so that the oil is 7 to 8 inches deep.

Heat the oil until it bubbles, and drop in 2 to 3 slices of cheese. They will sink to the bottom. Once they float to the surface, allow them to cook for a couple of minutes and then remove them with a slotted spoon.

Note: If the first piece browns too quickly when it is first dropped in the oil, add a little more oil to the pot to cool the oil down.

Marinara Sauce

2 to 3 tablespoons olive oil
6 cloves garlic
2 (28-ounce) cans whole, peeled Italian tomatoes, one can drained
3 tablespoons oregano
¾ teaspoon salt
½ teaspoon pepper
1 cup dry red wine
1 cup chicken broth

In a sauté pan, heat the olive oil and add the garlic.

Cook until the garlic is soft, and then crush it with a fork.

Add the tomatoes.

Add the oregano, salt, pepper, wine, and broth and cook uncovered on high heat until it is reduced by a little more than half, approximately 30 to 40 minutes. Continue to crush the tomatoes as they soften while cooking.

To serve, place each piece of cheese on a plate and top each piece with 3 or 4 tablespoons of marinara sauce.

Serve hot.

Success! The oil boils.

Dr. David gives Kit the first taste.

Crab Cakes and Corn Pudding

Serves 6 to 8

Crab Cakes

1 pound jumbo lump crabmeat
½ cup mayonnaise
2 large eggs, lightly beaten
2 teaspoons prepared Dijon mustard
¼ cup chopped fresh flat-leaf parsley
¼ cup chopped fresh dill
½ cup chopped red pepper
½ teaspoon salt
½ teaspoon freshly ground pepper
½ cup fresh bread crumbs

Drain the crabmeat and remove any bits of shell.

While the crabmeat is draining, mix the mayonnaise, eggs, mustard, parsley, dill, and red pepper in a bowl.

Add the drained crabmeat to the mayonnaise mixture and mix gently until combined.

Add salt and pepper.

Add enough fresh bread crumbs to the mixture to mold a "cake" with your hands. *Note:* The mixture should be more wet than dry.

Place each cake on a parchment-lined baking sheet and refrigerate for 1 hour.

Bake the crab cakes at 350°F for 20 to 30 minutes, or until nicely browned on top.

Corn Pudding

12 fresh ears of corn, husked
3 tablespoons unsalted butter
½ teaspoon freshly grated nutmeg
Salt and pepper to taste
½ cup heavy cream (optional)
½ cup water
¼ teaspoon salt
1 cup lima beans (fresh or frozen)

Score each ear of corn and cut off the kernels into a bowl.

With the back of a knife, using pressure, scrape the corn cob to extract as much of the "milk" as possible from the cob into the bowl with the kernels.

Heat a large sauté pan and melt the butter.

Add the raw corn and cook in the butter for about 15 minutes, stirring occasionally, and taste to make sure the "raw" flavor has been eliminated.

Add nutmeg, salt, and pepper. If the corn is too stiff, add some heavy cream sparingly.

In a separate small saucepan, boil the water and salt.

Add the lima beans and cook for 10 minutes, or until tender.

Toss the lima beans with the corn and plate a portion of the mixture under each crab cake.

Mile-High Blueberry Pie

Serves 6 to 8

Whipped cream and a scoop of vanilla ice cream finish this dessert deliciously.

Crust

2½ cups Graham crackers, crumbled, or 1 prepared Graham cracker crust
⅔ cup granulated sugar
½ cup (8 tablespoons/1 stick) unsalted butter, melted

Preheat oven to 350°F.

Pulse the graham crackers into crumbs in a food processor. Make enough crumbs to line a 9-inch pie pan.

Mix the crumbs and sugar in a medium bowl.

Add melted butter to the crumb-sugar mixture.

Combine well and press the mixture onto the bottom and up the side of the pie pan.

Bake crust for 10 minutes.

Remove the baked crust and let cool.

Filling

2 (11-ounce) jars fruit jelly or jam (I like a combination of blueberry and blackberry)
2 tablespoons fresh lemon juice
1½ envelopes unflavored Knox gelatin
2 pints fresh blueberries, washed and dried
Zest of 1 lemon
Cinnamon

Empty the jars of jelly into a medium saucepan and cook over low heat until it liquifies.

Add the lemon juice and gelatin and mix them into the melted jelly.

Remove from heat.

Add the blueberries, lemon zest, and cinnamon to taste.

Stir to incorporate.

After the mixture has cooled slightly, pour it into the cooked crust and refrigerate the pie for at least 3 hours before serving.

The proportions are fairly easy to divide. For every pint of blueberries, you need an 11-ounce jar of jelly, a tablespoon of lemon juice, and ¾ envelope of gelatin. If you need to increase the volume for a larger pie, you can do so accordingly. The gelatin keeps the pie firm and prevents oozing at serving time. Don't overdo it on the gelatin though, or your pie will be chewy as a rubber band!

Sunday Brunch

A simple table greets early-morning risers and invites them to start the day by serving themselves as they wish. A table set later for brunch usually includes the very colorful work by North Carolina ceramicist Stanley Mace Anderson. Stanley uses the majolica style of free-flow color and paints directly on the surface, giving the appearance that the maker has not labored painstakingly over the decoration. The splashes of color on every piece speak of an exuberance that is part of Stanley's decorative style.

The whimsical faces on the handblown goblets by William Bernstein are perfect for orange juice or parfaits. They make you want to smile back. Cornish Ware, in traditional blue and white stripes, completes the setting.

Stanley Mace Anderson plates, mugs, creamer, and sugar
Cornish Ware

William Bernstein goblets

Breakfast Parfaits

Makes 6 servings

This is an easy breakfast dish adapted from a recipe from Canyon Ranch. Depending on your choice of yogurt and cream cheese, you can adjust for calories versus taste. I'd go for the taste.

1 cup diced peaches
1 cup raspberries
1 cup blueberries
1 cup strawberries
¼ cup orange or cranberry juice
2 cups yogurt (Greek-style yogurt suggested)
3 tablespoons cream cheese (low-fat or regular)
½ teaspoon pure vanilla extract
3 tablespoons maple syrup
Mint leaves

Combine the peaches and berries in a bowl.

Lightly crush the fruit and add the orange or cranberry juice to them.

Combine the yogurt, cream cheese, vanilla extract, and maple syrup in another bowl and mix well.

Layer the fruit mixture with the yogurt into each of 6 parfait or stemmed glasses, ending with the fruit on top or some whole fresh berries that have not been crushed.

Garnish with a sprig of mint.

Serve cold.

Berkshire Mountains Granola

Makes a large canister, or 15 servings

When Leonard and I traveled to Lenox, Massachusetts, for a "destination wedding," we had the good fortune to stay at Stonover Farm, a charming inn. Innkeepers Tom and Suky have created a very special bed-and-breakfast experience for guests, having restored an 110-year-old Berkshire "cottage" that had been the farmhouse on the property of the Stonover estate. Suky's homemade granola awaits you when you walk into the kitchen in the morning, and Tom whips up creative omelettes and artisanal bacon.

The charm of the setting is matched by the charm of the owners, who had left a fast-paced life working in the music industry in Los Angeles to follow their dream to serve guests, with great pride for the life they have made in the heart of the Berkshire mountains.

Suky generously shared her wonderful granola recipe, which she serves for breakfast with yogurt and fresh fruit. I added slivered almonds and walnuts to her recipe, and, truth be told, I love it as much over ice cream!

8 cups organic rolled oats
2½ cups hulled sunflower seeds or slivered almonds and walnuts (or a combination of each)
2 cups pure maple syrup
3 tablespoons black sesame seeds
1 cup organic seedless raisins or combination of dried fruit

Preheat oven to 300°F.

Mix oats and sunflower seeds or almonds in a large bowl.

Add the maple syrup and mix well.

Spread mixture on two lightly greased cookie sheets and place in the oven for approximately 1 hour, stirring several times during baking to assure an even color.

When mixture is a golden brown, remove it from the oven and let cool.

Place the black sesame seeds in a sauté pan over low heat and sauté for 3 to 5 minutes, or until the seeds start to pop. (There is no need to put any oil in the pan; the seeds do not stick.)

Remove the seeds from the heat and place them in a large mixing bowl.

Add the oat mixture and raisins and mix ingredients thoroughly.

Transfer the mixture to a large, airtight container or canister and store in a dry place.

The granola will keep for several weeks.

Black sesame seeds are available in health-food stores or Asian markets. Dried fruit that has been cut into bite-size pieces—mangoes, apricots, or cranberries work well and add a little color—can be added in addition to or instead of the raisins, according to your taste.

French-Toast Casserole

Serves 6 to 8

1 loaf challah bread
10 eggs
1½ cups half-and-half
½ cup maple syrup
½ cup (8 tablespoons/1 stick) unsalted butter, melted
1 teaspoon pure vanilla extract
8 ounces cream cheese, cut into small bits (I prefer to use Philadelphia Cream Cheese)
1 to 2 tablespoons cinnamon
Butter for greasing the baking dish

Preheat oven to 350°F.

Pull challah loaf apart into bite-size pieces, or cut the loaf into cubes, and set aside in a large bowl.

In another bowl, beat eggs and add the half-and-half, syrup, melted butter, and vanilla extract, and mix well.

Pour the egg mixture over the torn bread and mix together well.

Pour the bread mixture into a greased 9 by 13-inch baking dish.

Smooth out the top and tuck in the bits of cream cheese, distributing them evenly.

Sprinkle cinnamon over the casserole.

Cover loosely with aluminum foil and bake for 30 minutes.

Remove the foil and continue baking for another 30 minutes.

Serve with warm maple syrup on the side.

Chocolate-Chip Bundt Cake

Serves 6 to 8

Many years ago, I came across a popular recipe for an easy Bundt cake made with a Duncan Hines cake mix and a package of instant pudding. This very-easy-to-make recipe produces a cake that is still moist the next day and that never reveals its simple store-bought ingredients.

4 eggs
1 box Duncan Hines Classic Yellow Cake Mix
    (not the butter-recipe golden cake mix)
1 cup sour cream
½ cup vegetable oil
1 package Jell-O Instant Vanilla Pudding
1 (12-ounce) bag Nestlé chocolate chips

Preheat oven to 350°F.

Mix all the ingredients except the chocolate chips in a bowl.

Beat for 4 minutes at medium speed.

Stir in half the bag (6 ounces) of chocolate chips.

Put the remaining chocolate chips in a food processor or blender and pulse until they become ground chips.

Add the ground chocolate chips to the batter.

Pour the batter into a nonstick Bundt pan (or a regular Bundt pan coated with cooking spray).

Bake for 50 minutes, or until a toothpick inserted into the cake comes out clean.

Allow the cake to cool in the pan for 30 minutes, then turn it out onto a serving plate.

Stanley Mace Anderson plates and mugs

Good Friends, Good Recipes
Toshiko Takaezu's Tossed Tofu

I first met Toshiko Takaezu after I fell in love with a beautiful pot in an exhibition organized by the Clay Studio in Philadelphia. Toshiko's Mo-Mo, a raku-fired, closed-form pot, remains one of my favorite ceramic works.

When I was interested in seeing more of Toshiko's work, she invited me for lunch at her home in nearby Quakertown. What a treat that was! Toshiko, who is a wonderful gardener as well as a renowned ceramist, took me through her vegetable patches and many rows of blooming perennials on our way to see her studio. Her studio contains a large kiln for firing pots, and it amazed me then, as it does today, that this tiny woman could handle the weight and the scale of those mighty, large forms.

After the visit to her studio, we went to her house. We entered the house from a porch and, following the traditional Japanese custom, we removed our shoes. The house held myriad treasures from other potters, weavers, and woodworkers, and I was fascinated by this part of Toshiko's artistic history. In her kitchen, I watched Toshiko weave magic with ingredients picked fresh from the garden that she plated and served at a lovely table set on her wooden deck overlooking her beautiful flowers. Summer was the perfect time of the year to be visiting Toshiko.

When I decided to write this book, I called Toshiko to ask her to contribute a recipe. She giggled and said that she never follows recipes; rather, she makes up recipes. Over the telephone, she described this wonderful dish she often serves.

Serves 8

1 brick tofu, cut into ¼-inch pieces
1 head Chinese cabbage (bok choy)
4 eggs
A lot of salt
A large bunch of chopped parsley

In the vegetable oil of your choice, fry the tofu until it is very brown.

Tofu is pretty bland tasting, so you have to sprinkle a lot of salt on it. Salt the tofu and continue to taste it as it cooks until it is seasoned to your liking.

Meanwhile, cut the cabbage into very fine pieces and "sneak" the cabbage under the tofu in the pan and sauté it until it is wilted and cooked through.

Beat the eggs and pour them over the tofu and cabbage and cook until the eggs are soft.

Sprinkle parsley on top before serving.

Toshiko Takaezu, *Mo-Mo*

Fall Back in the Country

Fall in the northeast part of the United States exhibits a hearty mix of brilliant colors. Besides the kaleidoscopic display of foliage that changes from green to fiery red to gold, a vivid palette is also created with seasonal fruits and vegetables: bright orange pumpkins, vibrant green zucchini, lush purple eggplants, and a dazzling range of red apples. Fall is the time of year when an outdoor farm market is itself a colorful exhibition space, with numerous wooden baskets displaying farm-fresh seasonal bounty. Exploring farmers' markets and feeling the first cool air of fall heightens the experience of seasonal change.

Fall is the beginning of holiday gatherings for our family, which start with celebrating the Jewish New Year, followed by Thanksgiving. It is a season for mealtime gatherings with heartier menus. It is also the season when the days get shorter and the feeling of eating good food triumphs over the thought of colder days ahead.

Menu
·
Poulet en Gelée
·
stuffed tomatoes
with
minted Peas
·
Pink Pears

Paula Winokur entry ledge

A Traditional Holiday

Rosh Hashanah is the holiday also known as the Jewish New Year, when we pause to take account of our lives and pray that we will enjoy a sweet and peaceful new year. On this holiday, Leonard and I host a traditional luncheon for dear friends, many of whom have families who live far away. After attending morning services at our individual synagogues, we sit down to the table to enjoy a meal that includes many sweet dishes, to ensure that our prayers for a sweet year will be heard.

For this holiday table, I like to mix my contemporary dinnerware with vintage pieces that belonged to my mother. Our tradition of combining family heirlooms and new tableware provides a timeless sense of continuity between generations and creates unique combinations for table settings.

I commissioned Joy Raskin to create the flatware for us after becoming acquainted with her work while I served as a juror one year for the Moss Rehabilitation Hospital's art show, which showcases the talents of artists who have overcome disabilities. Joy has a genetic condition that affects her hearing and sight. The Art Deco–inspired lines in the forks and knives she made are a fresh design for the classic period. She won a prize in the show, and later I contacted her about the commission.

The small plates are by Jill Bonovitz, a leading Philadelphia ceramic artist whose small porcelain sculptures are as wonderful as her paper-thin plates with intriguing designs. The dinner plates, cups, and saucers are by James Makins, whose work deliberately shows the beautiful random lines that his wheel leaves on each piece as he creates them. I don't know if there are many holiday lunches served on Makins's plates, but the lightly glazed white porcelain is a perfect background for this colorful meal. Adding to the table are antique plates that hold ceramic apples by Barbara Eigen. Removing the lid of the apple reveals the traditional honey used for dipping apples or challah bread.

The simple, elegant wine glasses blown by Smyers Glass are a lovely shade of deep pink—the perfect color for serving a traditional sweet red wine. The color of the glasses always brightens any table setting I plan, and white wine looks just as beautiful in these glasses.

The liver paté was presented in an Ingrid Bathe porcelain cup on a pear-shaped plate made by Barbara Eigen and served with a sterling-silver knife by Robyn Nichols.

The vintage plates used for dessert belonged to my mother. On this holiday, the mix of old and new couldn't be more appropriate.

Barbara Eigen ceramic apples
Smyers Glass wine glasses

Joy Raskin flatware

James Makins dinner plate

Jill Bonovitz plate

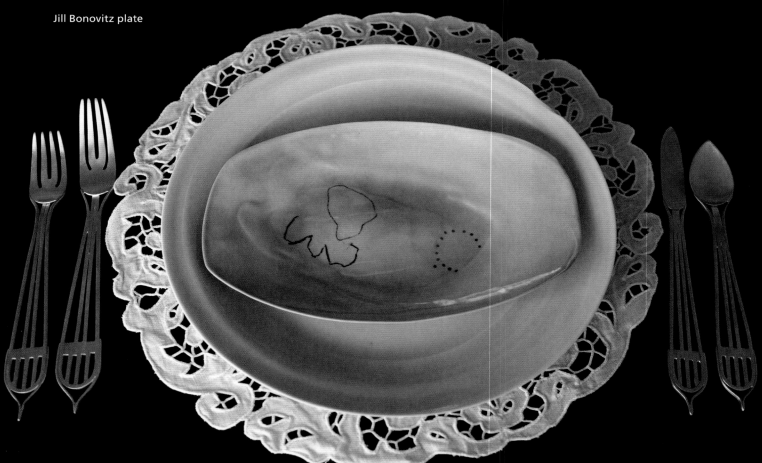

Dan Dailey candlesticks

Patrick Seegers crystal bowl

Chopped-Liver Pâté

Serves 12 as an hors d'oeuvre

Jayson Grossberg, who is a friend and a mighty fine chef, appeared at my door the day before Rosh Hashanah with a gift of his divine chicken-liver pâté. As we were waiting for everyone to gather on the holiday, I served the pâté with crackers and toast points. Later, to my delight, Jayson generously shared his recipe with me.

4 ounces port
1 pound chicken livers
1 hard-boiled egg, cooled and peeled
4 ounces diced, peeled apple
4 ounces diced onion
8 ounces cold unsalted butter
2 teaspoons apple-cider vinegar
2 tablespoons extra-virgin olive oil
Salt and freshly ground black pepper

In a nonreactive bowl, marinate the chicken livers in the port overnight.

Remove the chicken livers from the port and dry them with paper towels. Discard the port.

Cook the apple and onion in 1 tablespoon of oil until soft.

Sauté the chicken livers in 1 tablespoon oil.

Cool all ingredients.

Pureé all ingredients in a blender or food processor until smooth.

Season with salt and pepper to taste.

Barbara Eigen plate
Ingrid Bathe cup
Robyn Nichols knife

Rosalie's Doctored Gefilte Fish

Serves 12

Gefilte fish is a traditional food for the beginning of a Jewish holiday meal. Today there are two ways to prepare gefilte fish. One way is the lengthy, traditional way that our grandmothers followed, and the other is commonly called "doctored" gefilte fish. My mother, a thoroughly modern woman, decided to teach me her "doctored" way, as the memory of her own mother purchasing the fresh carp and keeping it alive in the bathtub until it was time for it to be prepared and cooked was probably not as important to her as the tradition itself.

3 large carrots, sliced into ¼-inch slices (about 1½ cups)
2 medium yellow onions
2 (24-ounce) jars of Manischewitz All Whitefish in jelled broth
2 tablespoons paprika
2 teaspoons freshly ground black pepper
2 tablespoons chopped parsley
1 (10-ounce) jar prepared red horseradish

James Makins dinner plate, Jill Bonovitz plate

Preheat oven to 375°F.

Place the carrots and onions in a large oven pan, and place the fish (6 individual pieces) with the jelled broth on top.

Sprinkle the fish with the paprika, pepper, and parsley.

Cover with aluminum foil and bake for 25 minutes.

Remove the foil and baste the mixture with the juice.

Bake for 10 more minutes, or until the carrots are tender and the paprika is slightly browned.

Allow the fish to cool or, if serving the next day, refrigerate overnight.

Serve with a tablespoon or two of horseradish.

Noodle-Pudding Soufflé

Serves 12

3 tablespoons unsalted butter or margarine, melted
¼ cup sugar
⅓ cup graham cracker crumbs
1 (8-ounce) package medium egg noodles, cooked and drained
6 tablespoons unsalted butter or margarine, softened
¼ cup sugar
6 ounces cream cheese, softened
1 pound cottage cheese
6 eggs, separated into yolks and whites
4 teaspoons sour cream
½ teaspoon salt

Preheat oven to 350°F.

Make the topping by combining the 3 tablespoons of melted butter with the sugar and graham cracker crumbs in a small bowl. Set aside.

Grease a 9 by 13-inch pan.

In a large bowl, combine the cooked and drained noodles, 6 tablespoons of butter or margarine, sugar, cream cheese, cottage cheese, egg yolks, sour cream, and salt. Set aside.

Beat the egg whites to stiff peaks, and gently fold them into the noodle mixture.

Pour the mixture into the greased pan and bake for 45 minutes.

Remove from the oven and sprinkle the crumb topping on top, and bake for 15 minutes more, or until golden.

Allow the pudding to cool slightly before cutting and serving it.

Tzimmes with Carrots, Sweet Potatoes, and Prunes

Serves 12

Tzimmes—a dish prepared with a sweet taste in mind—is traditionally eaten on Rosh Hashanah. The quantities of each ingredient depend on your taste; using a little less or a little more will determine how sweet you wish it to be.

1 bunch fresh carrots
6 medium sweet potatoes or yams
1 cup dried, pitted large prunes
1 cup orange juice
½ cup honey
½ teaspoon salt
3 tablespoons unsalted butter

Preheat oven to 350°F.

Cook the carrots and sweet potatoes in boiling salted water for about 15 minutes, or until cooked through but still firm.

Place the carrots and sweet potatoes in an oven-proof casserole and add the prunes, orange juice, honey, and salt and mix to combine.

Dot with the butter.

Bake uncovered for 45 minutes to 1 hour, stirring occasionally so that the juices are mixed throughout and the vegetables are soft but not mushy.

Beer-Baked Brisket

Serves 12

It seems there are as many beef brisket recipes as there are cooks! For this holiday meal, I have tried many recipes, and it seems that this one has received the best reviews. Keep in mind that this wonderful "comfort" dish is delicious served the day after it was cooked. Before reheating the brisket, remove any congealed fat and discard it. Slice the brisket while it is cold and place the portions in a casserole dish and cover them with the gravy. If the gravy is too thick, thin it with boiling water or beef stock. Bake in a 375°F oven for 20 minutes, or until the brisket is heated to the desired temperature.

1 8- to 10-pound first-cut brisket
3 large sweet onions, sliced in rings
6 stalks celery, cut in large chunks
3 whole carrots, cut in large chunks
2 packets dried onion soup mix
2 cups chili sauce
1 (12-ounce) bottle of beer
¾ cup water
Salt and freshly ground black pepper

Preheat oven to 350°F.

Pat the brisket dry, trim off any excess fat, and place it in a large ovenproof casserole or Dutch oven.

Place the onions, carrots, and celery on top of the brisket. Combine the dried soup mix with the chili sauce and water and pour the mixture over the brisket.

Pour the bottle of beer over the meat and sauce.

Cover with aluminum foil or a lid, place in the oven, and, basting often, cook for 2½ to 4 hours, or until the meat is tender.

Serve immediately or allow to cool completely, and then refrigerate overnight.

If serving immediately, slice the brisket on the bias, and pour a little of the gravy on each portion, reserving enough extra gravy to pass in a bowl around the table.

Grandmom Sarah's Strudel

Makes 24 pieces

My grandmother was a wonderful baker, and she never followed a written recipe. One day, many—many—years ago, in order to preserve her famous strudel for posterity, my sister, Reggie, and I decided to write down our grandmother's recipe on paper as we watched her cook. We stopped our 91-year-old grandmother at every step in the process so we could measure "a handful of this" or a "pinch of that." The result was successful, but we learned that the secret lay in her skilled hands, which patiently rolled, pulled, and stretched the strudel dough.

Long after our grandmother passed away, a wonderful picture of her still remains in my mind, and I am happy to have the memory of the day my sister and I eagerly gathered the ingredients from our grandmother, who remained somewhat puzzled by our desire to measure the ingredients. I think she knew that the secret to baking was in the hands.

Since I do not have the knack for kneading, I often substitute phyllo pastry sheets for the dough. I know my grandmother would approve.

Dough

5 cups sifted all-purpose flour
¼ teaspoon salt
⅓ heaping cup sugar
1 heaping teaspoon baking powder
½ cup Mazola oil
2 eggs, lightly beaten
1¼ cups water
3 tablespoons cinnamon
½ cup sugar

In a bowl, mix the flour, salt, sugar, and baking powder together.

Make a well in the dry ingredients, and add the oil, eggs, and water.

Knead the dough with your hands (do not knead with an electric mixer) until mixed well.

Refrigerate for 1 hour.

Divide the dough into four sections.

Knead each section, one at a time, on a floured wooden board or marble slab, into an oblong shape until each section is paper-thin.

Mix together the cinnamon and sugar.

Generously brush each section with vegetable oil and sprinkle with the mixture of cinnamon and sugar.

Filling

5 apples, peeled, cored, and coarsely chopped (a variety of apples works well)

1 cup coarsely chopped walnuts

¾ cup golden or dark raisins

2 tablespoons sweetened shredded coconut

1 (12-ounce) jar of strawberry jam, or other fruit jam

1 tablespoon fresh lemon juice

½ tablespoon grated lemon rind

½ cup fresh bread crumbs

1 tablespoon sugar

1½ teaspoons cinnamon

Preheat oven to 350°F.

Grease a large cookie sheet with butter.

In a bowl, mix the apples, walnuts, raisins, coconut, strawberry jam, lemon juice, lemon rind, cinnamon, and sugar.

Spread a long, thin mound of the filling on one long end of a sheet of dough.

Sprinkle thinly with bread crumbs and roll up the sheet of dough and filling.

Repeat with each sheet of dough until all the filling has been used.

Place the strudel rolls on the greased cookie sheet and cut each on the diagonal into two-inch-wide pieces.

Brush each piece lightly with oil and sprinkle with cinnamon and sugar.

Bake for 50 minutes, or until golden brown.

Curator's Lunch

One of my favorite lunchtime guests is David Revere McFadden, chief curator at the Museum of Arts and Design in New York. We always have many subjects to talk about: a new exhibition David is planning, a talented young artist that he has recently seen, or our favorite subject—food. Since David collects vintage Jell-O mold cookbooks and is an authority on the history of gelatins, a "poulet en gelée" was the perfect choice for a cold lunch. Although this lunch was planned for two, the recipes serve more.

With the meal plated on Mineo Mizuno's black-and-green dinnerware and set on a matching tablecloth and napkins that Mineo designed and had printed at Philadelphia's Fabric Workshop and Museum, the table was a balance of minimal design, with a splash of color visible in the stuffed tomato. The pitcher is by Akira Satake and the flatware—made in France—is by Laguiole.

Mineo Mizuno dinnerware and goblets
Fabric Workshop and Museum tablecloth and napkins
Akira Satake pitcher
Laguiole flatware

Poulet en Gelée

Serves 8

Typically suitable for a summer luncheon or light supper, this recipe is best if made and eaten within 48 hours, as the gelatin tends to get rubbery if it sits too long. The end result should look like a chicken mosaic in enough aspic to cover all the ingredients, including the lemon slices and tarragon leaves, dill, or parsley sprigs.

1 cup dry white wine
5 cups chicken broth (homemade or canned)
3 packets Knox gelatin
1 to 3 tablespoons fresh lime juice (to taste)
1 roast chicken (store bought is fine), skin removed and the meat cut into bite-size pieces
4 tablespoons green onion or scallion, sliced into ¼-inch pieces
2 tablespoons fresh tarragon, dill, or parsley
3 medium lemons, sliced into very thin rounds

Mix the wine and chicken broth together.

Pour 3 cups of the wine and broth mixture into a heatproof 4-cup liquid measuring cup set in a shallow pan of boiling water on the stovetop.

Pour the gelatin into the wine/broth mixture and stir constantly until the gelatin dissolves and the liquid is clear.

In a medium saucepan, heat the remaining 3 cups of the wine and broth mixture until hot. Add the hot gelatin/wine/broth mixture to it.

Add lime juice to taste and turn off the heat.

Ladle the liquid aspic into a 9 by 13-inch serving dish until it is ½-inch deep.

Refrigerate the aspic in the serving dish for 10 minutes, or until it sets.

Remove the dish from the refrigerator and arrange half the chicken, half the scallions, half the herbs, and half the lemon slices into a mosaic design on top of the ½-inch layer of chilled, set aspic.

Ladle another layer of aspic over the chicken layer, making sure you have enough aspic left for a third layer.

Chill the dish again for 10 to 15 minutes so that the aspic sets.

Remove the dish from the refrigerator and arrange the rest of your ingredients into the final mosaic layer and ladle the remaining aspic over it.

Refrigerate for at least 3 hours to chill throughout.

Remove the poulet en gelée from the refrigerator about a half hour before serving. The flavor is best if the aspic is not ice-cold.

For a quick and easy sauce on the side, mix equal parts of Heinz Chili Sauce with Hellman's Mayonnaise. Stir in enough capers, with a little juice from the jar, to complement the sauce and add a dash or two of Tabasco sauce, if you'd like.

Stuffed Whole Tomatoes with Minted Peas and Herb Mayonnaise

Serves 4

4 medium red tomatoes
14 ounces fresh or frozen baby peas
⅛ cup sour cream
⅛ cup mayonnaise
1 tablespoon lemon juice
1 tablespoon chopped scallions
¼ teaspoon salt
¼ teaspoon freshly ground pepper
½ tablespoon chopped fresh mint

For each serving, slice one tomato—keeping the stem end intact—into eighths, and gently open it to form a nest.

If using frozen peas, place them in a colander to defrost and drain any excess water.

Mix the peas with the sour cream and mayonnaise in a bowl.

Add the lemon juice and scallions and season with salt and pepper.

Add the chopped mint and mix well.

Fill each tomato nest with the pea mixture and chill until serving time.

Pink Poached Pears

Serves 4

I like to use Bosc pears—the best-shaped pear, with nice long, elegant stems.

2 cups red wine (I prefer Merlot, but any red varietal is fine)
2 cups water
½ cup sugar
2 tablespoons fresh lemon juice
1 (3-inch-long) cinnamon stick
4 ripe pears, peeled but with stems intact

Combine wine, water, sugar, lemon juice, and cinnamon stick in a medium saucepan.

Bring to a boil and then reduce the heat to a simmer.

Using a slotted spoon, place the pears in the pot and simmer them for 25 minutes, turning them often so that each pear absorbs the wine and turns a nice pink color.

Remove the pears from the pot and allow them to cool.

The pears can be served warm or can be made ahead of time and refrigerated to be served cold later.

Garnish each pear with a spoonful of vanilla ice cream or whipped cream and a sprig of mint, if desired.

A Gluten-Free Thanksgiving

Our daughter Suzy was diagnosed with celiac disease, an autoimmune digestive disorder that is triggered by the consumption of gluten, a composite that is typically found in wheat, barley, and rye. Therefore, celebrating a holiday that centers on food is always a challenge for her.

Because of the disease she lives with, Suzy often said that she had a love/hate relationship with Thanksgiving. She loved the holiday because it is such a happy family gathering, but she hated being deprived of all the wonderful traditional dishes we serve on that day. The answer to a menu that was safe for Suzy and that everyone would enjoy was simple: together, we developed dishes that were as delicious as the traditional Thanksgiving fare but didn't contain any gluten. And to everyone's satisfaction, we resolved the issue of serving turkey: I cook one turkey with traditional bread stuffing and another turkey—usually a large turkey breast—without stuffing. We are mindful to serve delectable dishes that are gluten-free, and Suzy's gluten-free pumpkin pie would rival any traditional homemade pie.

The traditional holiday plates we use were purchased in Italy, when, many years ago, we were traveling with a group from New York's American Craft Museum (recently renamed the Museum of Arts and Design) and visited a ceramics foundry in Faenza. Leonard and I were impressed with their beautiful production of stoneware and along with two other travelers decided to commission them to make us a set of plates that we could use for Thanksgiving. We wanted an image of a turkey to be painted on the plates. The language barrier presented a challenge as the potters did not speak English and our Italian was strictly Freshman 101. On the wall of the studio was a watercolor of a farm scene and a turkey running through a field. While pointing to the picture, and using sign language for placing the image of a turkey on the rim of the plate, we completed a successful commission. They are, however, the only Thanksgiving plates I have ever seen where some of the turkeys are running full tilt instead of calmly standing still.

In addition to the plates, the tables are set with a collection of raffia-and-straw Pilgrims and Native Americans and assorted straw turkeys and pumpkins in natural colors. Sometimes I spray small gourds with bright-gold paint and mix them on the table with shiny green Granny Smith apples. The water goblets and wine glasses are by Guy Corrie.

The assorted handblown candlesticks are by many artists. The large pot in the background is by William Daley, who lives and works in Philadelphia. Bill is regarded by many to be one of the most distinguished ceramic artists of the day. For over fifty years, his single focus has been to create vessels. Letters from Bill (I save them all) are always embellished with his drawings—often hand-colored—and filled with his thoughts about life, clay, and the human spirit. I am proud to call Bill a dear friend.

Guy Corrie water and wine glasses
William Daley pot
Plates made in Italy

Squash and Spinach Gratin

Serves 8 to 10

This is one of our favorite holiday dishes—a little labor intensive but certainly worth it.

6 large cloves of garlic, unpeeled
½ teaspoon extra-virgin olive oil
2 acorn squash (3 pounds total)
½ pound fresh spinach, ribs removed
1 teaspoon unsalted butter
½ teaspoon freshly grated nutmeg
Salt and freshly ground black pepper
2 teaspoons chopped fresh thyme
2¼ cups heavy cream
3 tablespoons gluten-free bread crumbs
⅔ cup freshly grated Parmesan cheese

Preheat oven to 450°F.

Place the unpeeled garlic cloves in an ovenproof dish or ramekin, drizzle with olive oil, and roast for about 20 minutes until light brown and very soft.

Let cool long enough to handle, then peel the garlic and cut into slivers; set aside.

Reduce oven temperature to 400°F.

Peel the acorn squash, cut each crosswise, and remove the seeds.

Cut the squash lengthwise into ¼-inch slices; set aside.

Steam the spinach until it wilts, then squeeze the excess water out of the spinach, chop the leaves roughly, and set aside.

Butter a 2½-quart baking dish and place half of the squash slices in the dish, saving the prettier ones for the top.

Sprinkle ¼ teaspoon of the nutmeg, ¼ teaspoon of salt, and ⅛ teaspoon of pepper on top of the squash.

Place half of the roasted garlic on top of the squash and sprinkle it with 1 teaspoon of the fresh thyme.

Arrange the chopped spinach over the squash and sprinkle it with ¼ teaspoon salt and ⅛ teaspoon pepper.

Place the remaining squash slices over the spinach and sprinkle with the ¼ teaspoon salt, ⅛ teaspoon pepper, 1 teaspoon thyme, and the remaining ¼ teaspoon nutmeg.

Distribute the remaining garlic over the squash, tucking it in between the slices.

Pour the heavy cream over the assembled gratin and cover the dish with aluminum foil.

Bake for 20 minutes, remove the foil, and press the squash down with a spatula to compress it and to distribute the liquid.

Re-cover the dish with the foil and continue baking for 20 minutes.

While the squash is baking, combine the bread crumbs and Parmesan cheese in a bowl.

After the gratin has baked for the second 20 minutes, reduce the oven temperature to 375°F and sprinkle the bread crumb and cheese mixture over the squash.

Bake uncovered about 10 to 15 minutes longer, or until the gratin is golden brown.

This dish can be prepared in advance. To reheat, simply cover the gratin loosely with aluminum foil and reheat in a 375°F oven for 20 minutes. Remove the foil after 20 minutes, sprinkle with ½ teaspoon of fresh thyme, and continue baking for another 10 minutes, or until hot and golden brown.

Carrot Soufflé

Serves 8 to 10

6 cups cooked, sliced carrots (approximately 4 pounds raw carrots)
1 cup sugar
6 tablespoons gluten-free flour
2 teaspoons baking powder
1 cup butter, softened
6 eggs, beaten

Preheat oven to 400°F.

Mash the cooked carrots and place them in a large mixing bowl.

Mix the sugar, flour, and baking powder together in a separate bowl.

Add the dry ingredients, butter, and eggs to the carrots and combine the mixture well, either by hand or with a mixer.

Pour the mixture into a greased shallow casserole dish, cover with aluminum foil, and bake for 15 minutes.

Reduce the oven temperature to 350°F, remove the foil, and bake the soufflé uncovered for 45 minutes.

The soufflé is finished when a toothpick inserted into the center comes out clean.

Robert Farrell serving piece

Creamed Onions

Serves 12

In our house, creamed onions have always been a favorite dish for Thanksgiving, so we converted a traditional recipe to a gluten-free recipe, and nobody at the table can tell the difference.

4 pounds unpeeled white pearl onions
2½ teaspoons salt
6 tablespoons unsalted butter
2 tablespoons white rice flour
2 cups half-and-half or heavy cream
½ teaspoon freshly grated nutmeg
½ teaspoon freshly ground pepper
1½ cups gluten-free bread crumbs

Preheat oven to 350°F.

Blanch the onions by plunging them into boiling water for 1 minute, removing them from the boiling water, and immediately plunging them into a bowl of cold water to stop the cooking.

When they are cool enough to handle, peel the onions.

Put the onions back into a pot, cover them with cold water, add the salt, cover the pot, and bring them to a boil.

Reduce the heat to simmer and cook the onions about 20 to 25 minutes, or until they are tender.

Drain the onions well and put them in a buttered casserole dish.

In a saucepan, melt the butter over low heat.

Whisk in the flour, add the half-and-half or heavy cream, and whisk until smooth.

Add the nutmeg and pepper to the flour mixture and simmer for 2 minutes. Pour the liquid over the onions in the casserole and sprinkle with the bread crumbs.

Bake for 30 minutes and until the sauce bubbles.

Karen Karnes salt-glazed and wood-fired pots

Apple-Cranberry Cobbler

Serves 12

8 to 10 apples, peeled, cored, and chopped into
    bite-size pieces
¾ cup fresh cranberries
5 teaspoons fresh lemon juice
1 teaspoon gluten-free pure vanilla extract
½ cup maple syrup
1 teaspoon ground cinnamon
1 cup quinoa flakes or gluten-free rolled oats
½ cup coconut oil

Preheat oven to 375°F.

Place the apples and cranberries into a 9 by 13 by
2-inch baking dish.

Mix together the lemon juice and vanilla extract,
pour over the apples, and stir the mixture to
combine.

In a medium bowl, combine the maple syrup, cinnamon, and quinoa or oats.

Stir in the coconut oil.

Pour the mixture over the apples.

Bake 45 to 50 minutes, or until the topping is crisp
and golden brown.

Pumpkin Pie

Makes 1 pie

Crust

½ cup white rice flour
¼ cup cornstarch
¼ cup potato starch
1½ teaspoons sugar
¼ teaspoon salt
¼ cup cold unsalted butter, cut into cubes
1 large egg, lightly beaten
1 to 2 tablespoons cold water
1 large egg yolk, beaten

In a large bowl, combine the rice flour, cornstarch, potato starch, sugar, and salt and whisk until mixed well.

Cut the cold butter into the flour mixture, using a pastry cutter or a fork.

Add the egg and 1 tablespoon of water and stir until the mixture comes together and forms into a dough. Stir in the other tablespoon of water if the dough seems dry.

Gather the dough, form into a ball, and wrap with plastic wrap.

Chill the dough in the refrigerator for at least an hour, or overnight.

To roll out the piecrust, remove the dough from the refrigerator and allow it to sit at room temperature for 15 minutes.

Place the dough on a piece of plastic wrap or parchment paper and cover with another piece of plastic wrap or parchment. Roll out the dough to a circle approximately 12 inches in diameter.

Place the crust in a 9-inch pie plate and crimp the edge.

Brush the edge of the crust with beaten egg yolk and set the unbaked crust aside.

Filling

1 (15-ounce) can pure pumpkin
1 (12-ounce) can evaporated milk
¾ cup packed dark brown sugar
2 large eggs
1½ teaspoons ground cinnamon
½ teaspoon ground ginger
½ teaspoon salt
¼ teaspoon ground cloves
¼ teaspoon ground nutmeg

Preheat oven to 350°F.

In a large mixing bowl, combine all the pie-filling ingredients and blend with a mixer for about 2 minutes.

Pour the filling into the prepared piecrust.

Bake for 50 to 55 minutes, or until the center no longer wiggles, remove from the oven and cool on a wire rack.

Serve while warm or, when completely cool, store covered in the refrigerator.

Decoration (optional)

1 egg yolk, lightly beaten
1 teaspoon sugar

To make cutouts for decorating the pie, simply use the cookie cutters of your choice.

Brush dough pieces lightly with egg yolk, sprinkle lightly with sugar, and bake the dough "cookies" on a cookie sheet in the oven while the pie is baking.

The cutouts will be golden brown after about 15 to 20 minutes.

Remove them from oven, cool, and use to decorate the pie when it is finished baking.

Timeless Tradition Party

When our grandchildren were younger, we initiated a family holiday party that we called "Family Appreciation Night," which celebrated our appreciation for each other. Each of us picked a family member's name out of a hat, but instead of buying a gift for that person, we wrote a few lines about how we appreciate them. Clever poems were written and lovely pictures drawn, all of which were presented at a family gathering two weeks later. We had a lot of fun during the process and, of course, a dinner party was planned for the presentation of the creative endeavors.

For one of these family parties, I set the table with our collection of antique hourglasses. The collection, which was begun by my father, represents the "sands of time." While the sand moves through the neck of the hourglasses, we concentrate on the day we are gathered together. The sand in the top of the hourglass represents the future we cannot predict, and the sand below represents the past we should not dwell on. The hourglasses represent the timelessness of tradition and the timelessness of a family. The collection of hourglasses continues to grow as friends find excellent sources for us in antique shops in the United States and abroad.

The popovers, baked in multicolored wine cups made by Sheilagh Flynn, greeted everyone as they sat down to a dinner of osso buco served on stoneware plates made by Liz Kinder. The water glasses are vintage Depression glass, which emphasized the timelessness theme. For dessert, profiteroles were served in glass fruit bowls that were placed on laser-cut plastic plates made by Koziol Design, adding a note of contemporary technology in tableware.

As the years went on, the appreciation tributes got more sophisticated, but the warmth of the family, food, and night still endured.

Sheilagh Flynn ceramic cups
Liz Kinder plates

Popovers

Makes 12

Popovers have always been a family favorite to make and eat. I recall one grandson pulling a stool up to the oven and sitting and watching through the glass oven door for 30 minutes as the popovers we had just prepared doubled in size. We had discussed the importance of keeping the oven door closed until the popovers rose. He was very patient!

1½ **cups all-purpose flour**
1½ **tablespoons salted butter, melted**
3 large eggs
½ **teaspoon salt**
1½ **cups whole milk**

Preheat oven to 450°F.

Whisk the flour, butter, eggs, salt, and milk until smooth.

Grease a muffin pan very well, then fill each cup halfway with the batter (the popovers rise when baked).

Bake for 30 minutes. It is important not to open the oven door during the baking time; this will cause the popovers to fall.

Popovers are best served immediately, while they are warm.

You can serve popovers with a flavored butter, such as an herbed butter for a savory meal or a strawberry butter if you are serving the popovers for brunch.

Sheilagh Flynn cups

A few of the hourglasses from our collection

Osso Buco and Meyer Lemon Risotto

Serves 12

Osso Buco

12 veal shanks (the thick hind shanks are the meatiest)
1 cup all-purpose flour
Salt and freshly ground black pepper
1 cup extra-virgin olive oil
1 cup unsalted butter
2 large onions, coarsely chopped
6 large garlic cloves, peeled and chopped
1 teaspoon dried basil
1 teaspoon dried oregano
4 cups beef stock
2 (28-ounce) cans Italian plum tomatoes, drained
3 cups dry white wine
½ cup chopped flat-leaf Italian parsley
Grated zest of 1 lemon
4 anchovy fillets packed in oil, mashed (optional)

Preheat oven to 350°F.

Place the flour in a large bowl and season it with salt and pepper.

Dredge the veal shanks well in the flour.

Heat the oil and butter in a large ovenproof casserole over medium heat, and brown the shanks for five minutes on each side.

Remove the shanks and place them on paper towels to drain.

Add the onion, garlic, basil, and oregano to the casserole and cook until the onion is softened but not brown.

Stir in the stock, and cook for another 10 minutes, then skim the excess fat from the mixture.

Add the wine and cook another 15 minutes.

Season with salt and pepper.

Return the veal to the casserole, cover the casserole with a lid, place it in the oven, and bake for 1½ to 2 hours, or until the veal is tender. Add more stock while baking if the liquid has reduced too much; the finished stew should be thick.

Before serving, sprinkle the stew with parsley, lemon zest, and mashed anchovies.

Meyer Lemon Risotto

Serves 6

Missy Keyser, a personal chef, introduced me to this wonderful risotto, which I think is a perfect match for Osso Buco. The Meyer lemons add a delightful snap to the risotto.

3 tablespoons extra-virgin olive oil
2 shallots, chopped
1 teaspoon fine-grain sea salt
2 cups lightly pearled barley

½ cup white wine

6 cups heated water, vegetable stock, or a combination of both

2 Meyer lemons, cut into cubes, rind removed and reserved

¼ cup Meyer lemon juice

Heat the olive oil in a large, heavy saucepan over medium heat, add the shallots and salt, and sauté, stirring often, until the onions begin to soften.

Add the barley and stir until coated.

Add the white wine and simmer for 3 to 4 minutes, or until the barley has absorbed the liquid.

Add 1 cup of the water or stock; adjust the heat to maintain a gentle, active simmer; and let the barley absorb the liquid.

Add 1 cup of the water or stock and let the barley absorb the liquid. Repeat until all 6 cups have been added and absorbed, stirring regularly so that the grains mix and cook through as they absorb the liquid. This should take 30 to 40 minutes.

When the barley is tender, remove the saucepan from the heat.

Finely mince the reserved lemon rind and mix 3 tablespoons of the rind with the lemon juice and barley.

Add salt to taste.

Garnish with the lemon cubes.

Liz Kinder plate

Profiteroles

Serves 4 to 6

My favorite dessert is profiteroles—cream puffs filled with ice cream and topped with hot fudge sauce. What could be a better ending to any meal? This classic recipe for cream puffs will serve 4 to 6, but it is easy to double. The empty cream puffs freeze well, and if you slice them in half before freezing them, it is easy to take them out of the freezer, fill each half with ice cream, and top them with your choice of warm chocolate sauce. I always feel that "if it is not chocolate, it's not dessert!"

½ cup butter
⅔ cup water
1 cup all-purpose flour
½ teaspoon salt
4 eggs

Preheat oven to 450°F.

Grease a large cookie sheet.

In a pan, heat the butter and water together and bring to a boil.

Remove the pan from the heat and add the flour all at once, stirring vigorously until a ball forms in the center of the pot.

Cool slightly.

Add one egg at a time, beating hard after each addition. The dough should be shiny.

Using a tablespoon, drop individual dollops of dough onto the greased cookie sheet.

Bake at 450°F for 5 minutes.

Reduce the oven temperature to 350°F and continue baking for 15 minutes, or until the puffs are golden.

Koziol Design plate

When the puffs are cool, slice them in half, fill each half with ice cream—or fill one half and top with the other half—and top with hot fudge or chocolate sauce.

Although it is not a classic finish for profiteroles, fresh whipped cream on the top is delightful.

Good Friends, Good Recipes
Elisabeth Agro's Full-Circle Gefilte Fish

Elisabeth Agro and I became immediate friends in 2006 when she was appointed the Nancy M. McNeil Associate Curator of American and Contemporary Crafts and Decorative Arts at the Philadelphia Museum of Art. I was thrilled that the museum had named a dedicated curator for modern and contemporary crafts because few museums have endowed such a curatorial position, and Elisabeth's curatorial history at the Carnegie Museum in Pittsburgh, Pennsylvania, was outstanding.

Elisabeth and I have had many conversations about the past and present state of the craft world, the artists we find interesting, and the goals of the museum's crafts exhibition program and permanent collections. One day, while we were enjoying a cup of tea in my kitchen, I revealed to Elisabeth my plans for writing a book that documented my collections of handmade dinnerware and favorite recipes. That was the moment when Elisabeth shared the history of her relationship with her mother-in-law, and how making gefilte fish in her mother-in-law's kitchen became a vehicle for bridging her acceptance into her husband's family. Recalling Rosh Hashanah, and its significance of renewal and redemption, she wrote this story about her life with her mother-in-law as a prelude to sharing the recipe.

Renewal, Redemption, and Rosh Hashanah
By Elisabeth Agro

Judaism, its holidays and rituals, became intractably linked to my life over twenty-three years ago when I fell in love with Rob, a nice Jewish boy from Long Island. I was not Jewish, and, as sometimes can happen, reception into a family of another faith can be complicated. These early years were sometimes difficult. I yearned for Rob's mother's acceptance and unconditional love.

At my first Rosh Hashanah as Rob's fiancée, I arrived at his parents' house bearing a gift for his mother, Sheila—a scarf with an Asian carp/circle of life motif that I intentionally chose to coordinate with the significance of the holiday. Sheila told me that Rosh Hashanah was her favorite holiday. We spoke about renewal, referencing her gefilte fish and the carp that goes into making it.

In the most difficult of times, her kitchen became my haven, where her ambivalence about my non-Jewish heritage was cast aside while we prepared and cooked the next holiday meal for eager and hungry relatives. In Sheila's kitchen, she and I found and shared a common language and love of food. At her kitchen counter I learned to make several traditional Jewish delicacies, including the following recipe for gefilte fish.

In preparation for our first Rosh Hashanah after Sheila's death, I was determined to make her recipe for gefilte fish in order to envelop our house with familiar scents of the holiday to comfort Rob and ease his sadness over the loss of his mother. I made over 125 fish patties and fish soup so thick it would have made Sheila cry with pride!

Reflecting on my first Rosh Hashanah without her, I realize that she and I had come full circle on that sweetly saddened holiday. Like the circle of life motif on the scarf, our relationship had transformed through a cycle of renewal and redemption.

Full-Circle Gefilte Fish

Makes 24 to 30 patties

When ordering the fish from the fishmonger, have them grind the whitefish, pike, and carp together for you. Make sure they reserve the heads, skin, roe, and all bones and have them throw in a few extra fish heads if possible; you will need them for the broth.

Broth

Reserved fish heads, skin, roe, and bones
2 large onions, chopped
5 carrots, sliced
Salt and black pepper
Sugar, to taste

Place the fish heads, skin, roe, and the bones with the onions, carrots, salt, pepper, and sugar in a large soup pot, cover with water, and cook for 1½ hours.

Strain the broth into a clean pot and reserve the carrots.

Fish Patties

2 carrots
2 large onions
1 celery stalk
6 large eggs
¼ cup matzo meal
Salt and white pepper
Ice water
8 pounds combined ground whitefish, pike, and carp

In 6 batches, process the carrots, onions, and celery in a food processor. With each batch, add an egg, matzo meal, salt and pepper, and enough ice water to lightly moisten the mixture.

Mix all batches together and adjust the salt.

With wet hands, shape the fish mixture into patties and set aside.

In a large pot, bring the broth and reserved carrots to a rolling boil.

Add the fish patties and cook for 1½ hours.

Remove the fish patties and carrots and transfer to a serving platter.

Cool before serving.

Winter Under the Palm Trees

The construction of our new home on the east coast of Florida provided us with the opportunity to seek out innovative craftsmen who would play a central role in creating important design features of the house. We first commissioned Wendell Castle, the celebrated American furniture artist, to design the front doors and Albert Paley, a renowned metal sculptor, to design the entrance gates. The planning stage with Castle and Paley—discussing the constraints associated with the property, the need for architectural compatibility with the house, and our desire for the theme of palm trees in the designs—was a joyful process that was matched only by watching the final installation of these great treasures.

We gave Wendell, a longtime friend ever since the days he and I attended American Craft Council board meetings together, the challenge of creating front doors that would harmonize with the cast-stone and horizontal aluminum bands on the exterior of the house. His solution was a pair of eleven-foot-tall doors that are metal on the exterior but reveal the same design, carved from mahogany, on the interior. The magnificent doors blur the lines between sculpture, furniture, and architecture—the signature of Wendell's work.

We have always admired Albert Paley's bold, architectural sculptures, which we had seen in a variety of regional landscapes, where he had bent and stretched metal and suggested organic root-like structures in his designs. Having a Paley work of our own became our dream, and the realization of that dream are his monumental, welcoming gates celebrating the tropical Florida climate. The gates are consistent with his unique sculptures, which triumphantly blend architecture and sculpture.

While planning the architectural features of our house, we acquired a colorful, exuberant wall sculpture by Betty Woodman that fills our combined kitchen and family room with joy every day.

Wendell Castle and me outside the front doors

Wendell Castle's doors, inside

Original drawing of the gates by Albert Paley

Albert Paley gates at the entrance to the driveway

Betty Woodman wall installation

Patrick Loughran plates
Robert Mickelsen wine glasses
Michael Schunke wine glasses
Ginny Ruffner candlesticks
Lisa Jenks salt and pepper shakers
Mardi-Jo Cohen flatware

Winter Menus

Super Bowl Kitchen Supper

The inspiration for a kitchen supper came from the wonderful dinnerware made by Minnesota-based Will Swanson. Will works in stoneware as well as porcelain, and the rustic glazes, combined with the heavy weight of his stoneware plates and bowls, characterize the craftsman's handmade process. His earthy dinnerware seemed perfect to use at our kitchen table on the evening that we watched the Super Bowl, and the casual tone of the night was set.

The first course I served was gougère, a dish I learned to make as a newly married woman when I took a cooking course from Madeleine Kamman, a superb French cook who, in her Philadelphia home, taught the basics of traditional French cuisine. I can still hear her French accent as she taught her students many exciting culinary tips she had learned from her days at Le Cordon Bleu in Paris.

Will's bowls hold a generous helping of the one-dish meal Chipotle-Spiked Chili, which was simply complemented by crusty French bread. While we were enjoying dinner, it was easy to bake a lemon soufflé, another recipe based on one by Madeleine Kamman, and to serve the dessert hot out of the oven and before the game was over.

The table is set with "moonshine cups" made by multimedia artist Micah Sherrill. On the outside of each wonderful cup, he has provided a unique texture, and on the inside, a colorful glaze. Aside from enhancing most any table setting, Sherrill's cups feel very comfortable in your hand.

Will Swanson plates
Micah Sherrill cups

Gougère

Serves 8

Gougère is a regional pastry from the Burgundy region in France and can be eaten cold or warm. I prefer it warm, right out of the oven. It makes a wonderful cocktail-time snack, especially when served with a glass of red wine.

½ cup water
½ cup whole milk
7 tablespoons unsalted butter, cut in small pieces
1 teaspoon salt
¾ cup sifted all-purpose flour
4 eggs, lightly beaten, plus 1 lightly beaten egg for glazing
¼ cup grated Gruyère cheese
¼ cup diced Gruyère cheese
Pinch of nutmeg
Pinch of cayenne pepper (optional)

Preheat oven to 375°F.

In a pot, mix water, milk, butter, and salt and slowly bring to a boil.

When the mixture foams, remove it from the heat and slowly add the flour, a little at a time.

Put the pot back on the heat and continue to whisk the mixture until a ball of dough forms in the pot, all the liquid has been absorbed, and the batter has pulled away from the sides of the pot.

Add the four beaten eggs, a little at a time, and the grated Gruyère cheese and cayenne.

Grease a baking sheet with butter. Spoon the batter into a wide wreathlike ring, brush the wreath with the beaten egg, and press the diced Gruyère lightly into the top of the batter.

Bake at 375°F for 35 to 40 minutes, or until the wreath is well-browned.

Cut the wreath into wedges and serve with drinks.

Instead of making the traditional wreathlike ring, you can spoon the dough into 15 to 20 individual gougères and bake them at 375°F for 35 to 40 minutes.

Nina's Chipotle-Spiked Chili

Serves 8

During the months that we reside in Florida, it is a delight to secure the help of Nina Cioffi. Affectionately known to us as Chef Nina, she assists me in creating delicious meals when Leonard and I host dinner parties. Nina's wonderful recipes, combined with my tried-and-true dishes, and her concern for the presentation of food have enabled us to create many memorable dinners.

1 cup sifted all-purpose flour
¼ cup plus 1 tablespoon chili powder
2 teaspoons chipotle powder
2 tablespoons ground cumin
3 tablespoons paprika
3 pounds boneless beef chuck, cut into ¾-inch cubes
⅓ cup light olive oil
1½ large sweet onions, chopped (about 2½ cups)
1 tablespoon minced garlic (I prefer to use elephant garlic)
3 large carrots, chopped
1 tablespoon dried oregano, crumbled
1 tablespoon dried hot red pepper flakes, or to taste
2 (8-ounce) cans tomato sauce
1¼ cups beef broth
3 tablespoons cider vinegar
2 red bell peppers, seeded and chopped
1 (19-ounce) can kidney beans
1 (19-ounce) can black beans
Salt and freshly ground black pepper
½ cup shredded sharp cheddar cheese
½ cup crème fraîche or sour cream
1 cup chopped scallions

Chef Nina and her pot of chili

In a medium bowl, mix the flour, 1 tablespoon chili powder, 1 teaspoon chipotle powder, 1 tablespoon cumin, and 1 tablespoon paprika.

Coat the beef cubes with the flour mixture. Shake off any loose flour from each piece.

Warm the olive oil in a Dutch oven over medium-high heat and add the beef cubes.

Brown the beef cubes on all sides.

Transfer the beef to a plate and set aside.

Add the onions to the pot and cook over moderately low heat, stirring occasionally, until soft.

Add the garlic and carrots, stir the mixture, and cook for 1 minute.

Add the oregano, red pepper flakes, and the remaining chili powder, chipotle powder, cumin, and paprika, stir, and cook for 1 minute.

Add the beef back to the pot along with the tomato sauce, beef broth, vinegar, and half the chopped red bell pepper.

Bring to a boil, then lower the heat, cover the pot, and simmer for 2 to 3 hours, or until the beef is tender.

Add the beans, the remaining chopped red bell pepper, and salt and pepper to taste.

Simmer uncovered for 15 minutes, or until the peppers are tender.

To serve, place the chili in individual serving bowls and garnish with shredded cheddar cheese, crème fraîche or sour cream, and scallions.

If a spicier dish is preferred, add more chipotle powder, or stir chopped chipotle peppers in with the shredded cheese.

Lemon Soufflé

Serves 6

*Madeleine Kamman had definite thoughts on souf-
flé making. She noted that French dessert soufflés
are almost always served without a sauce, and their
centers are kept very soft and creamy. Although I
have followed her recipe for Grand Marnier Soufflé
over and over again, it is this recipe, based on her
Lemon Soufflé, that I find light enough to complement a dinner of chili and elegant enough to add a
little surprise to a kitchen party.*

1 large lemon
4 teaspoons cornstarch
¾ cup milk
3 teaspoons unsalted butter
4 egg yolks, beaten lightly
6 tablespoons granulated sugar
6 egg whites
Pinch of salt

For the topping
1 tablespoon superfine sugar
1 tablespoon confectioners' sugar

Preheat oven to 375°F.

Prepare an 8-inch soufflé dish by heavily greasing
the interior bottom and sides of it with vegetable
oil and dusting it generously with coarse granulated sugar. Shake off the excess sugar and set the
dish aside.

Grate the lemon peel into a fine zest and set aside.

Squeeze the juice out of the lemon into a saucepan.

Add the cornstarch and whisk until smooth.

In a separate saucepan, scald the milk and mix it
carefully into the lemon and cornstarch mixture.

Stir the mixture over low heat until it comes to a
boil and allow it to boil for 2 to 3 minutes, stirring
continually.

Add the butter, a little at a time.

Add the lemon zest.

In a separate bowl, beat the egg yolks and granulated sugar together until very light and fluffy, and
slowly add the mixture to the sauce.

In a separate bowl (use a metal bowl, if possible),
beat the egg whites and the salt until very stiff.

Fold the egg whites carefully into the lemon
mixture.

Fill the prepared soufflé dish to its top with the
mixture, and sprinkle the soufflé with superfine
sugar.

Place the dish in a pan of hot water that covers
approximately half of the soufflé dish and bake
at 375°F for 40 to 45 minutes, or until firm to the
touch.

Remove from the oven, dust with confectioners'
sugar, and serve at once.

Will Swanson plates

Dinner for Eight

Dinner at Eight was the name of an exhibit that my partner and I held at our gallery, Sign of the Swan, in Chestnut Hill, Pennsylvania, in 1985. In that exhibition, we featured many craftsmen who produced functional dinnerware. One outstanding ceramicist in the show was Patrick Loughran. After the show, I purchased his eight place settings for my personal use. Patrick recently told me that the dinnerware is now "vintage" and that for the past 18 years he has been teaching at the École Nationale Superieure d'Art in Limoges, France, and making sculpture in his studio. I am even more appreciative of this rare set of dinnerware today.

Now, when having eight for dinner, I have the opportunity to use the plates with handblown wine glasses by Robert Mickelsen. His graceful stemware depicts sea horses and dolphins, a theme that reflects Robert's love for the ocean. I incorporated another set of glasses on the table, each stem containing a unique spiral and graceful bowl, blown by Michael Schunke. The inclusion of his stemware on the table was fascinating because it allowed the settings to vary.

Ginny Ruffner is a celebrated glass artist whose numerous public and private commissions have fascinated museum visitors and collectors for many years. She recently made the ribbon candlesticks for an auction at the Museum of Arts and Design in New York City. The gracefulness of the design was so irresistible that I stood by the silent-auction table until the sale of the lot closed! Every time I see her wonderful work on my table, I am thankful that I persisted with my bidding.

The salt and pepper shakers are by Lisa Jenks, a jewelry maker whose beautiful work is well known. Less often seen are her extraordinary creations for the table. The salt and pepper shakers I set on my table are designed in a variety of shapes, and the golden glow of the metal glistens in candlelight.

We waited patiently for Mardi-Jo Cohen, an extraordinary metalsmith, to design and make a set of flatware for us. It was well worth the wait; the table sparkles with the beautiful forks and knives, which incorporate nonprecious stones. I feel like the table is adorned with jewelry.

Patrick Loughran plates and bowls
Robert Mickelsen wine glasses
Michael Schunke wine glasses
Ginny Ruffner candlesticks
Lisa Jenks salt and pepper shakers
Mardi-Jo Cohen flatware

Heirloom Tomatoes and Burrata Cheese

Serves 8

Unlike popular standard varieties of tomatoes, heirloom tomatoes are generally developed by organic-gardening and seed-saving practices and, like heirloom roses, have often been passed down through generations.

Nina introduced me to burrata, a fresh Italian cheese made from mozzarella and cream. The outer shell is solid mozzarella. When you slice it, you find a soft, creamy interior made of mozzarella and cream. This rich, buttery-flavored cheese is not always easy to obtain because it must be eaten soon after it is purchased, but a good market resource can usually order it for you. Of course, a fresh mozzarella can substitute for burrata.

4 medium yellow heirloom tomatoes
4 medium red heirloom tomatoes
2 large balls burrata cheese (can substitute fresh mozzarella)

For the vinaigrette
1 cup extra-virgin olive oil
⅔ cup fresh or bottled lemon juice
2 tablespoons prepared Dijon mustard
2 tablespoons finely minced shallots
1 tablespoon chopped fresh parsley
1 tablespoon chopped fresh chives
Salt and freshly ground black pepper
Fresh basil, chopped (optional)

Combine all ingredients for the vinaigrette and set aside.

Slice the tomatoes and cheese.

On each plate, place one red tomato slice on a plate and top it with a slice of the burrata cheese, followed by a slice of yellow tomato. Follow with another slice of burrata on top and then a slice of red tomato. Drizzle some of the vinaigrette on top of the tomatoes and cheese and allow it spill onto the plate. Finish the arrangement by topping it with the chopped basil.

Duck Breasts with Farro Risotto

Serves 8

Duck Breasts

6 (8-ounce) boneless duck breasts, skin on

For the marinade
¾ cup chopped shallots
1 cup red wine
¼ cup chopped fresh rosemary
1 teaspoon sea salt
2 tablespoons soy sauce

Mix the shallots, wine, rosemary, sea salt, and soy sauce in a large bowl.

Place the duck breasts in the marinade, cover the bowl, and refrigerate for several hours or overnight.

Preheat oven to 375°F.

Remove the duck from the marinade and pat dry with paper towels.

Season the duck breasts with salt and pepper.

Cook the duck breasts, skin side down, in a heavy skillet until crisp and browned (about 4 minutes). Turn the breasts over and cook for another 4 minutes.

Place the breasts in an ovenproof dish and bake for 8 to 10 minutes, or until the breasts are cooked through. The duck should reach 150°F on an instant-read thermometer.

Remove the duck breasts from the oven and slice them. Arrange the slices in a fan-shaped arrangement around the farro risotto on each plate.

Long-stem artichoke hearts are an attractive addition to the plates.

(continued)

Farro Risotto

Farro can be found in Italian supermarkets or at most fine gourmet grocers.

2 cups farro
8 cups water
½ cup plus 1 tablespoon fruity olive oil
6 tablespoons butter
1 cup chopped sweet onions
2 garlic cloves, chopped
2 cups chicken broth
Seeds of one pomegranate (if pomegranates are out of season, use 1/2 cup dried cranberries instead)
½ cup capers, rinsed and drained
½ bunch fresh Italian parsley, chopped
Salt and freshly ground black pepper

Soak the farro in cold water for 20 minutes; drain and rinse.

Bring the water to a boil in a saucepan.

Add the farro and 1/2 cup olive oil, and simmer for 20 minutes.

Drain and rinse the farro in a strainer.

In a medium saucepan over medium heat, melt 4 tablespoons butter for about 3 minutes, or until almost brown, and add the remaining tablespoon of olive oil.

Add the onions and garlic and sauté for 1 minute.

Add the farro.

Simmer, stirring frequently, for about 5 minutes, or until almost all the liquid evaporates.

Add the chicken broth 1 cup at a time and simmer, stirring frequently, for about 14 minutes total, or until the liquid is absorbed and the farro is tender.

Add the pomegranate seeds, capers, and parsley and stir to combine.

Season to taste with salt and pepper.

Chocolate Bread Pudding

Serves 8

This recipe was given to me by Philadelphia's Leslie Rosen Catering. After a beautiful dinner party that Leslie catered for us, I received rave reviews for the dessert, and she generously shared the recipe with me. Leslie modified an original recipe by Anne Rosenzweig.

1 large loaf brioche or challah bread
4 cups heavy cream
2 cups semisweet chocolate chips
1½ cups sugar
10 egg yolks
1 tablespoon pure vanilla extract

Preheat oven to 350°F.

Butter a 9 by 13 by 2-inch baking dish.

Cut the bread into cubes and set aside.

In a heavy saucepan, heat the cream until a slight film forms on top.

Turn off the heat, and stir in the chocolate until it melts. Cool slightly.

In a separate bowl, whisk the sugar, egg yolks, and vanilla together.

Slowly whisk the cream and chocolate mixture into the egg mixture.

Stir in the bread cubes and let the mixture rest for 1 hour.

Pour the mixture into the buttered baking dish and cover with aluminum foil. Punch several small holes in the foil to allow the steam to escape.

Bake for 50 minutes.

You can make the pudding mixture ahead of time and refrigerate it for up to one day. Be sure to bring it back to room temperature before baking it.

Come for Lunch and Bridge

Most bridge luncheons are designed for four or eight people so that you have an even number of players. When you have many good friends you want to include, a card party becomes a challenge!

My plan was to serve lunch at the dining-room table, using blue-and-white plates in a variety of beautiful patterns that Leonard and I had purchased many years ago from a small shop in Ho Chi Minh City in Vietnam. Because I am uncertain of the clay content and whether they are food safe, I use them only as service plates. The cobalt-blue plates I have by British ceramicist Maryse Boxer are definitely food safe, and their wonderful high-gloss finish provided a great background for the coconut cake I served for dessert. The goblets are from Mexico, and although it is sometimes disconcerting to drink from them because their rims curve outward and you worry that the liquid is going to dribble down your chin, I often overlook impracticality when the design is pleasing.

Nina prepared a wonderful menu that began with two different melon soups, which she ingeniously poured into one bowl. Soup was followed by a niçoise salad made with chicken instead of tuna. Dessert was planned to be set on a side table and to be served while we were playing bridge, but the conversation around the dining table was so much fun that dessert was served at the table and the start of the bridge game delayed.

Maryse Boxer cobalt-blue glazed plates

Two-Melon Soup

Serves 9

1 large ripe cantaloupe, peeled, seeded, and cut into 1-inch cubes
1 tablespoon fresh lemon juice
1 tablespoon fresh orange juice
½ large honeydew melon, peeled, seeded, and cut into 1-inch cubes
2 tablespoons fresh lime juice

In a blender, puree the cantaloupe with the lemon and orange juices until smooth.

Transfer the cantaloupe puree into a container and refrigerate, covered, for several hours so that it is well chilled.

In a clean blender container, puree the honeydew melon and lime juice.

Put the honeydew puree in a covered container and refrigerate, covered, for several hours.

When you are ready to serve the soup, put each puree in separate pitchers or measuring cups and simultaneously pour equal amounts of the purees into a large serving bowl. The two soups will stay separated.

Composed Salad Niçoise with Chicken and Tarragon Vinaigrette

For each individual plate

Substituting chicken for the traditional tuna in a classic niçoise salad gives it a nice twist for a warm-weather luncheon.

2 small red-skin potatoes, boiled until tender and cut into wedges
½ cup French string beans (haricots verts) or small green beans with stems removed
1 small tomato, cut into wedges
1 hard-boiled egg, cut into quarters
½ breast of boneless and skinless chicken, cooked and sliced
Bibb lettuce or watercress
Pitted black olives
3 anchovies (optional)

Tarragon Vinaigrette
2 teaspoons prepared Dijon mustard
½ cup red-wine vinegar
1½ to 2 cups extra-virgin olive oil
¼ cup dried tarragon
Salt and freshly ground black pepper

For the vinaigrette, combine all ingredients in a bowl and whisk until blended.

To serve the salad, place ingredients for each plate in heaping sections on dinner plates and dress with the vinaigrette.

Coconut Cake

Serves 8 to 10

3⅓ cups sifted all-purpose flour (not self-rising)
1 tablespoon baking powder
1½ cups whole milk
½ teaspoon salt
1½ teaspoons pure vanilla extract
⅛ teaspoon pure coconut extract
1½ cups (3 sticks) unsalted butter, softened
1½ cups sugar, plus ¼ cup sugar
7 egg whites, at room temperature for 30 minutes
1 cup sweetened shredded coconut flakes

Frosting
2 cups confectioners' sugar
1 cup (2 sticks) of salted butter, softened
1 teaspoon pure vanilla extract
1 teaspoon pure coconut extract
3 tablespoons heavy cream

Garnish
Unsweetened coconut flakes, toasted or untoasted

Preheat oven to 350°F.

Grease the interiors of three 9 by 2-inch cake pans.

Line each pan with a round of parchment paper and then butter the paper.

Flour the pans, knocking out the excess flour.

In a medium bowl, sift together the flour, baking powder, and salt.

In another bowl, mix the milk and extracts.

In a third, large bowl, use a mixer at medium speed to beat the softened butter and 1½ cups of sugar until pale and fluffy, or for about 3 minutes.

Switch to low speed and add the flour mixture in three batches, alternating each batch with the milk mixture and mixing until incorporated.

In another large bowl, beat the egg whites with clean beaters at medium speed until they hold soft peaks.

Beat in the remaining ¼ cup sugar, 1 tablespoon at a time.

Continue beating until the whites hold stiff, glossy peaks.

Stir one-third of the egg-white mixture into the batter, and fold in the remaining mixture carefully but thoroughly.

Fold in the sweetened coconut.

Spread the batter evenly in the prepared cake pans and rap pans lightly on a counter several times to eliminate air bubbles from the batter.

Place two pans on the upper rack of the oven and one pan on the lower rack, and bake for 20 minutes.

Maryse Boxer plate

Switch the positions of the pans and bake about 10 to 15 minutes more, or until golden. Test for doneness by inserting a wooden toothpick in the center of each cake. When the toothpick comes out clean, the cakes are done.

Cool the cakes in their pans on cooling racks for 5 minutes.

Run a knife around the edges of the pans, and invert the cakes back onto the cooling racks.

Discard the parchment paper and cool the cakes completely, about 1 hour.

To make the frosting, beat the confectioners' sugar, butter, and extracts in a large, deep bowl with a mixer until light and fluffy. Stream in the heavy cream while continuing to beat the frosting.

To assemble the cake, place one cake layer on a cake stand or large plate.

Spread ½ cup of the frosting on top of the layer and smooth it out.

Gently place the second cake layer on the first, add another ½ cup of the frosting to the top, and smooth it out.

Add the third cake layer and frost the top of it with another ½ cup of the frosting.

Place the entire cake, uncovered, in the freezer and let set for about 30 minutes.

Remove the cake from the freezer, and frost the sides of the cake.

Sprinkle unsweetened coconut flakes over the top of the cake and press into the frosting on the sides.

Fraternity Brothers Reunion

In the winter, Florida is a perfect place for the University of Pennsylvania's Phi Epsilon Pi class of 1957 to have a reunion. Over many years, Leonard's "brothers," their wives, and the two of us have continued to enjoy meeting—alternating between the East and West Coasts—once or twice a year. In March, the warm, sunny weather of Florida becomes the destination of choice, giving Leonard and me the opportunity to catch up with old friends in a relaxed, enjoyable evening at our home.

The loggia works well for setting a long table to seat our many guests. A leopard skin–printed cloth, combined with dinnerware that Jeanne Bisson and Ikuzi Teraki of Romulus Craft designed for the new house, provided a colorful setting. The combination of Ikuzi's Japanese heritage and Jeanne's defined aesthetic produces distinctive tableware, using Ikuzi's own porcelain recipe. The colors were planned for the warm climate: terra cotta–colored plates with a high-gloss cream-colored "puddle" in the center, and the reverse of the colors on smaller plates. Large, black plates; honeycombed bowls; and demitasse cups and saucers accentuate the tropical palette of the setting.

Micah Sherrill's cups complement Romulus Craft's dinnerware beautifully. The "moonshine cups" look wonderful, feel comfortable, and are so interesting that we use them in many settings, including our Super Bowl Kitchen Supper (page 162).

Of course the menu for this reunion in Florida had to include Florida stone crab claws.

Romulus Craft plates and bowls
Micah Sherrill cups

Florida Stone Crab Claws with Honey-Mustard Sauce

Serves 10

Allow five stone crab claws per person for a first-course appetizer. It is easiest to have your seafood vendor crack the claws for you ahead of time, but be certain to serve them the same day. A fresh wedge of lemon and honey-mustard sauce for dipping make the dish memorable.

Honey-Mustard Sauce
1 cup mayonnaise
½ cup Florida orange-blossom honey
¼ cup white-wine vinegar
1 tablespoon tamari
½ cup prepared Dijon mustard
2 large bunches fresh tarragon (about 1 ounce total)
¼ cup light olive oil

50 stone crab claws
2½ lemons, cut into wedges

To make the mustard sauce, place all the ingredients except the olive oil in a food processor and blend for about 45 seconds, or until combined.

Slowly pour in the olive oil and blend to combine.

The mustard sauce can be made ahead of time and stored in the refrigerator for up to a week.

For each serving, arrange 5 crab claws in a small bowl on top of a few tablespoons of mustard sauce, or place the crab claws on a flat plate and serve the sauce on the side with a lemon wedge.

Vodka-Tossed Cherry Tomatoes

Serves 10

The vibrant color of this dish enhances any meat entrée. The tomatoes can be slightly cooked through—which is the way I like them—or cooked longer until some of them burst open a bit.

5 pints cherry tomatoes, rinsed, dried, stems removed
¼ pound sweet salted butter (or 4 tablespoons of butter and 4 tablespoons of olive oil)
¼ cup vodka
Salt and freshly ground black pepper

Melt the butter, or heat the butter and olive oil, in a skillet.

Add the tomatoes to the skillet and sauté over high heat for 3 to 4 minutes, stirring to make sure all the tomatoes are sautéed well.

Add the vodka and cook another 2 minutes until the alcohol reduces.

Season with salt and pepper and serve immediately.

Fillet of Beef

Serves 10

1 4- to 5-pound fillet of beef (whole beef tenderloin)
Salt, pepper, and garlic powder, to taste

Preheat oven to 425°F.

Trim any large deposits of fat off the top of the beef and thoroughly season the fillet with salt, pepper, and garlic powder on both sides. Place the fillet on a broiler rack or shallow roasting pan, fat side up.

Roast for 10 minutes.

Reduce heat to 350°F and roast for 25 minutes for rare meat (120°F on a meat thermometer) or 35 minutes for medium (130°F).

Remove the roast from the oven, cover it with aluminum foil, and let it stand for 10 minutes before slicing.

The individual salt and pepper ramekins by Akira Satake sit up on tiny feet and make excellent alternative containers for any sauce served with the beef. Here, the containers are filled with a mixture of sour cream, prepared horseradish, and chopped green onions. One-half cup sour cream to 1 tablespoon horseradish makes a good beginning. Add chives or chopped scallions for flavor, as well as color, and salt and pepper to taste.

Akira Satake ramekin

Strawberry Sorbet

Serves 10

When traveling to England, with our two grand-children, we visited a fraternity bother and his wife who have taken up residence there. Not only do they boast a llama farm, where they breed the stately animals, and a garage with antique cars (of his fraternity years' vintage), but they are very gracious hosts and great cooks. It was on that occasion that Henry introduced our grandchildren to a Pimm's Cup (page 90) and Ordell served her wonderful sorbet after a delicious dinner. Ordell was delighted when the children accepted second helpings, and I was delighted when she shared her recipe with me.

1 cup water
¾ cup sugar
¼ cup fresh lemon juice
½ cup fresh orange juice
2 egg whites
1 cup pureed strawberries

Steven Maslach glass

Combine the water and sugar in a saucepan, bring the mixture to a boil over high heat, and stir and cook it for about 5 minutes. Allow it to cool for a few minutes.

Stir in the lemon and orange juices, and pour the mixture into a shallow dish, bowl, or freezer tray. Freeze for 1 hour.

In a metal bowl, whip the egg whites until stiff.

Put half the frozen juice and sugar mixture into a food processor or blender and mix until smooth.

Add the beaten egg whites and process just long enough to mix the ingredients.

Add the pureed strawberries, mix well, and return the mixture to the freezer for 2 hours, or until it is solid.

I served the sorbet in handblown glasses by Steven Maslach, and I added a couple of pieces of chocolate-dipped tropical fruit to further enhance the Florida theme.

Shades of Green

The idea for the theme Shades of Green came from a new set of dinnerware made by Liz Kinder. I found Liz's work in a very twenty-first-century way—via the Internet. Up until then, I had only purchased work from craftsmen who I came across through exhibitions, galleries, craft shows, or street fairs.

I had selected Liz's Polka Dots pattern from her website, but I needed to choose the colors. Thinking about using these plates in Florida, I decided green would be compatible with the yellow walls in our house. Liz was concerned that we select the right green glaze. So Liz and I met to look at green color samples. I chose two greens to be used with the pattern, and within a month, my beautiful new green plates and bowls arrived.

Shades of Green was an obvious theme for a dinner beginning with a cold pea soup and ending with Key lime pie.

The table setting is composed of goblets by Robert Dane in mixed colors that celebrate the beauty of life in the Berkshire Mountains in Massachusetts, where he lives and works and gains daily inspiration. A green ceramic pitcher by Sandra Belcher served as a centerpiece. The stacked salt and pepper shakers and creamer and sugar are by Peter Saenger.

The quail-eggs appetizer was served on a laser-cut metal tray by Israeli artist Talila Abraham, and the cocktail glasses are the wonderful Tutti-Frutti raised-cane design by Robert Dane.

Liz Kinder plates and bowls
Robert Dane goblets
Sandra Belcher pitcher (used as a vase)
Peter Saenger salt and pepper shakers, creamer, and sugar

Truffled Quail Eggs

Serves 4

12 quail eggs
5 tablespoons white vinegar
4 yolks from hard-boiled large free-range chicken
**   eggs**
1 tablespoon prepared Dijon mustard
1 bunch baby chives, snipped to a quarter-inch
Salt and pepper to taste
1 tablespoon white truffle oil

Robert Dane glasses, Talila Abraham tray

Place the quail eggs and vinegar in a saucepan and fill with cold water, enough to cover the eggs. Bring to a boil and cook for 3 minutes.

Remove the pot from the heat.

Drain the water from the pot and add cold water, shaking the pot until the shells crack.

Peel the eggs, cut a sliver from the bottom of each egg so they stand up, and arrange on a platter.

Cut a small slice off the tops off the quail eggs to flatten the tops.

In a food processor, blend the egg yolks from the hard-boiled chicken eggs with the mustard, half of the snipped chives, salt, and pepper.

Slowly stream in the truffle oil.

Put the yolk mixture in a pastry bag with a small tip or into a plastic bag with a corner edge cut off.

Squeeze the yolk mixture onto the top of the quail eggs.

Garnish each egg with a piece of snipped chive.

Minted Pea Soup

Serves 4

3 tablespoons vegetable oil
2 cups finely chopped onions
1 (10-ounce) box frozen spinach, thawed
4 cups chicken stock
3 cups fresh peas (or frozen peas, thawed)
1 small bunch fresh mint leaves, stems removed
1 cup buttermilk (or heavy cream, if you prefer a thicker soup)
Salt and freshly ground black pepper

Liz Kinder plate and bowl

Heat the oil in a large pan.

Add the onions and cook over high heat until soft. Meanwhile, squeeze out the excess water from the spinach, and add the spinach to the onions.

Add the peas and chicken stock, bring to a boil, and continue to simmer about 10 minutes, or until the peas are soft.

Add mint leaves and pour half the mixture into a blender or food processor, reserving some of the liquid.

Process and set aside.

Blend or process the remaining mixture. Add it to the first mixture and stir in the buttermilk (or cream). Add any reserved liquid until the desired consistency is reached. Serve warm or refrigerate for 1 hour and serve chilled.

Shredded carrots and mint leaves make a pretty topping.

Bronzini

Serves 4

4 whole bronzini or sea bass, boned and scaled
    but with head and tail intact
2 tablespoons extra-virgin olive oil
2 lemons, sliced
3 tablespoons chopped fresh dill
4 sprigs parsley
½ teaspoon salt
½ teaspoon freshly ground black pepper
Zest of 1 lemon, chopped

Liz Kinder plate

Preheat oven to 400°F.

Rinse the fish and pat dry with paper towels.

Open each fish, skin side down, and drizzle each piece with olive oil. Stuff 2 or 3 slices of lemon, half the chopped dill, and a parsley sprig inside each fish and close.

Place fish on a lightly oiled baking pan. (You will probably need two pans to accommodate four fish.)

Brush the outside of each fish with olive oil and season with salt, pepper, and lemon zest.

Bake for 5 minutes. Turn the fish over and bake another 5 minutes.

Turn the oven to broil and cook the fish for 3 to 5 minutes, or until the skin blisters and the fish flakes easily with a fork.

Remove the fish from the oven and transfer it to serving plates.

Sprinkle the remaining dill over the fish for extra color before serving.

In many markets, bronzini is often called Mediterranean sea bass. The fish is also nice to serve over a bed of arugula with white asparagus.

Key Lime Pie

Serves 8 to 10

I asked my friend Judy, a very good cook, to test this recipe for me. I suggested that it could be written with an option of using a premade piecrust, but that didn't please my friend, who is a purist. She felt the pie was so delicious that it deserved a good crust. I wish I were more of a purist; I more often opt for quick and easy.

Crust
2½ cups graham cracker crumbs
⅔ cup sugar
¾ cup melted butter

Filling
8 egg yolks
2 (14-ounce) cans sweetened condensed milk
1½ cups Key lime juice
Grated rind and zest of 2 Key limes

Preheat oven to 350°F.

In a large bowl, mix the graham cracker crumbs, sugar, and melted butter until blended well.

Press the mixture into the bottom and sides of a 10-inch pie pan and bake for 6 to 8 minutes. When finished, remove from the oven and let cool.

Beat the egg yolks with the condensed milk. While stirring, add the Key lime juice.

Add the grated Key lime rind and zest and pour the mixture into the cooled crust.

Bake for 8 to 10 minutes at 350°F.

Chill several hours before serving.

Fresh whipped cream and a few Key lime slices make this dessert even more green.

Good Friends, Good Recipes:
Betty Woodman's Turkish Eggplant Ratatouille

In the early 1980s, I became aware of Betty Woodman's work when I purchased one of her "Pillow Pitchers" from the Helen Drutt Gallery in Philadelphia. That purchase began a love affair with Betty's work and a friendship with her that has continued to grow over the years. Betty's inventive use of color and glazes on her Pillow Pitchers started the development of her vase and vessel motif that has earned her international recognition.

Betty's ceramic wall installation in our house in Florida has the same painterly style and eccentric shapes and wild use of color as her vessels.

Betty, like so many craftsmen, is as comfortable in her kitchen as she is in her studio. While traveling in Italy one summer, Leonard and I had the very good fortune to visit Betty and her husband, photographer George Woodman. When we accepted an invitation for lunch at the Woodmans' home, located on a picturesque hillside in Antella, a small town on the outskirts of Florence, I realized the vibrant influences that surround Betty's work.

After touring Betty and George's studios, Betty stepped unnoticed into the kitchen and came out with a repast of homemade pasta with local bread and cheese, and George poured us local wine. The beautiful meal was served under an arbor overlooking the gorgeous hills of Florence. Is it any wonder that Leonard and I thought we were in heaven?

Serves 12

4 medium to large eggplants (or 10 to 12 Japanese [skinny] eggplants)

3 to 4 medium red onions

4 gnarly peppers: 2 yellow and 2 red are preferable, but one color is OK (do not use Holland bell or green peppers)

3 pounds fresh in-season tomatoes, cooked and sieved, or 1 (12-ounce) can Italian plum tomatoes with puree

1 large bunch fresh basil leaves, chopped
1 tablespoon coarse salt
Pinch fresh thyme leaves
Pinch fresh marjoram leaves

Preheat oven to 375°F.

Wash and cut the eggplants into 1 by 1-inch pieces.

Quarter and slice the onions (not too finely).

Cut the peppers into 1 by 1-inch pieces.

Put the eggplant, onion, and peppers in a large baking dish (an earthenware baking dish is best).

Add the tomatoes over the tops of the other vegetables, and stir in the basil, salt, thyme, and marjoram.

Cover tightly with aluminum foil and bake for 2½ hours.

Uncover, stir, and continue baking for another 1½ hours, stirring every 30 minutes or so until the mixture becomes thick and dense.

As a first course, the ratatouille may be eaten hot, tepid, or cold with a ladleful of plain yogurt and a handful of chopped Italian parsley on top, or it can be used as a pasta sauce, which is very good with a handful of olives thrown in. For breakfast, put a bit of olive oil on the bottom of a low, open casserole dish and add the cooked ratatouille to about 1 inch deep. Reheat in the oven at 350°F to 375°F. When it bubbles, pour beaten eggs (as many eggs as you have guests) on top. Put it back in the oven and bake for about 20 minutes until the eggs are set. Sometimes it is helpful to tilt the baking dish after the edges of the eggs have set to help cook the center. Another delicious variation is to add sliced mozzarella and goat cheese with the eggs. —B.W.

Betty Woodman, *Pillow Pitcher*

A Birthday Celebration—
A Work of Art

More than just a dinner party, this surprise birthday celebration for Leonard turned out to be a "happening." The event took place at the Norton Museum of Art in West Palm Beach, Florida, and the theme for the black-tie evening was A Work of Art.

Cocktails were served in a gallery of sculptures that were actually live mimes. When guests made their way to another gallery for dinner, they were invited to choose among three different cold soups served in shot glasses.

The dining tables were illuminated by slowly rotating streams of colored light from fixtures in the ceiling, while the table centerpieces were large, clear columns, each with a ball of carnations at the top.

There were many toasts and skits by friends; a Céline Dion look-alike (actually, "she" was a man, a drag queen who thoroughly fooled everyone) who crooned to the guest of honor; and a "Hats Off" performance—the big hit of the night—by our children and grandchildren, each one wearing a hat that represented their relationship to their father or grandfather.

The pastry chef orchestrated a brilliant dessert by creating edible paintbrushes—including bristles—out of pastry dough. Each guest was served a paintbrush and small scoops of various flavors of ice cream on a large dessert plate to resemble a painter's palette.

It was a fantasy party that became a memorable event.

Cucumber Tzatziki

Makes 8 quarter-cup servings

At the birthday party, this dish served as a light bite for guests while they sipped a cocktail. The presentation was very appealing; on a large tray, cucumber slices were arranged checkerboard style, and cucumber rounds were placed on the overlapping slices. Be creative in how you choose to serve this hors d'oeuvre.

1 cucumber, peeled and coarsely chopped or grated
2 tablespoons salt
1½ cups Greek yogurt
3 garlic cloves, crushed
2 tablespoons chopped fresh dill
1 tablespoon chopped fresh mint
2 tablespoons extra-virgin olive oil
1 tablespoon red-wine vinegar
4 cucumbers, peeled and sliced into rounds for the arrangement
Bunch fresh Italian flat-leaf parsley

Place the chopped cucumber in a bowl, sprinkle it with the salt, and let it stand for 30 minutes.

Rinse the cucumber under cold water to remove the excess salt.

Place the cucumber in a colander or strainer to drain, and squeeze the excess liquid from the cucumber a handful at a time.

Put the cucumber in a bowl and add the yogurt, garlic, dill, mint, oil, and vinegar, and stir until evenly mixed.

To serve, spoon the mixture onto the cucumber slices and garnish with fresh parsley leaves.

The filling can be made ahead of time, covered with plastic wrap, and refrigerated until ready for use.

Resource Guide

The following craftsmen make objects
for the table.

Abraham, Talila
metalaceart.com

Anderson, Stanley Mace
piedmontcraftsmen.org

Aram, Michael
michelaram.com

Aumann, Karen
kaumann@ccp.edu

Bathe, Ingrid
ingridbathe.com

Bernstein, William
bernsteinglass.com

Bloom, Roberta
artsleagueoflowell.org

Bonovitz, Jill
jillbonovitz.com

Boxer, Maryse
maryseboxer.com

Cecula, Marek
info@marekcecula.com

Charney, Jack
jjcharney@gmail.com

Cohen, Mardi-Jo
mardijocohen.com

Corrie, Guy
unionstreetglass.com

D, Samy
samy-d.com

Dailey, Dan
studio@dandailey.com

Dane, Robert
danegallery.com

Darwall, Randall
randalldarwall.com

Dayan, Vered Tandler
veredt@netvision.net.il

DiGangi, Joseph
digangidesigns.com

Eigen, Barbara
eigenarts.com

Farrell, Robert
farrellsilver.com

Flynn, Sheilagh
flynnclaystudio.com

Hafner, Dorothy
dorothyhafner.com

Halpern, Gina Rose
ginarosehalpern.com

Ivankovic, Michelle
greendepot.com

Jenks, Lisa
lisajenks.com

JRB Linens
jrblinens@verizon.com

Karros, Alec
akardesign.com

Kinder, Liz
lizkinder.com

Lane, Danny
dannylane.co.uk

Langsfeld, Liz
langsfeld.wordpress.com

Lurie, Elizabeth
elizabethlurie.com

Makins, James
jamesmakins@yoworks.com

Maslach, Steven
stevenmaslach.com

Mickelsen, Robert
rm@mickelsenstudios.com

Naples, Lisa
lisanaples.com

Nichols, Robyn
robynnichols.com

Pearce, Simon
simonpearce.com

Pinkwater Glass
pinkwaterglass.com

Raskin, Joy
spoonladyjr@juno.com

Reese, Claudia
studio@cera-mix.com

Romulus Craft
romuluscraft.com

Ruffner, Ginny
ginny@ginnyruffner.com

Saenger, Peter
saengerporcelain.com

Satake, Akira
akirasatake.com

Schunke, Michael
michael@nineironstudios.com

Sherrill, Micah
micahsherrill@googlepages.com

Smyers Glass
smyersglass.com

Swanson, Will
willswanson.com

Wainwright, Michael
michaelwainwright.com

Yuki, Yoshiaki
yoshiakiyuki.com

Index

Recipes

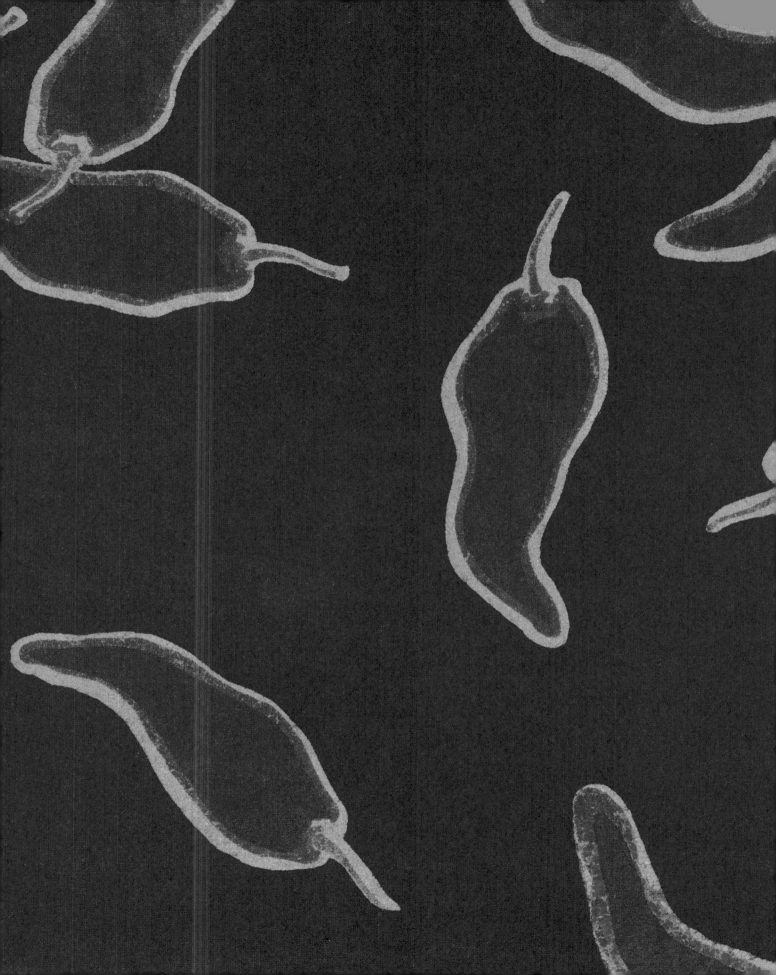

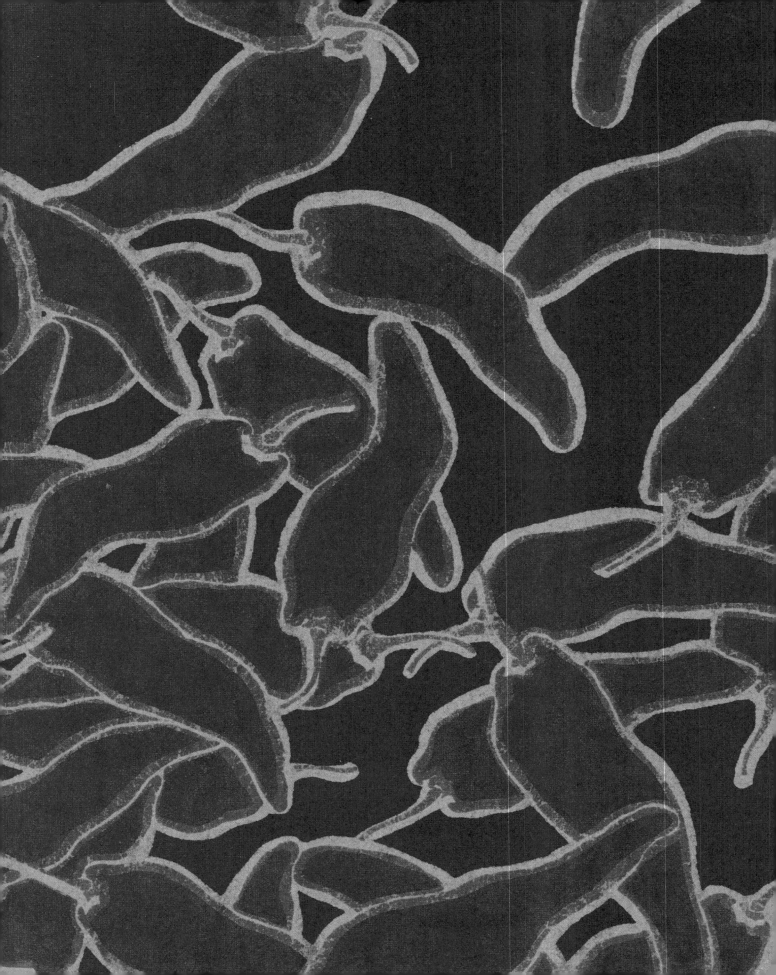